Who is my neighbour?

March 31

The "Sound of Music" was for all of us to enjoy at leisure.

This one is for me to ponder…In WWII (I was told), I was a baby in a dugout in Sibuga, Sabah, as people were hunkered down for fear of the bombs. At this moment in time, we are all isolated for fear of COVID-19. During the dark days of WWII, C. S. Lewis held a series of BBC radio talks broadcast, the provenance of his book "Mere Christianity." When the Great Plague ravaged through Britain beginning in 1665, Isaac Newton was a student at Trinity College, Cambridge. A few months after his undergraduate degree, the 23-year-old (for fear of the plague) retreated in isolation to his family farm. Newton wrote a series of papers called "fluxions," now known as "Calculus" during this time in isolation. The Apostle Paul, under house arrest for two years wrote most of the "New Testament" (Acts 28:16-30). I do not understand the appearance of this causative virus, SARS-CoV-2.

April 2

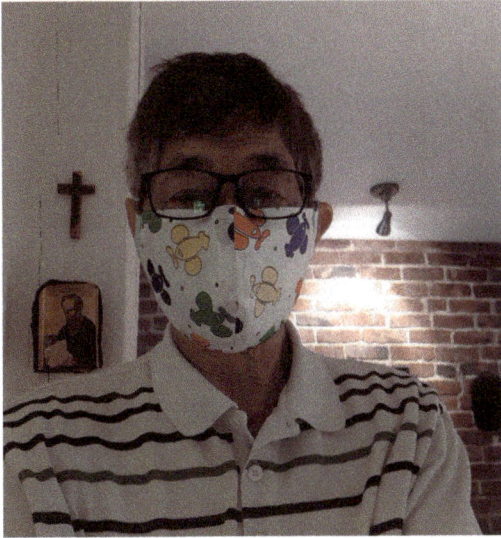

Despite its controversy, May is making face masks. Some in the past few days have thought (and will probably continue to think) of the fragility of life and that life is not what it seems. Some continue making a loud noise at one end and no sense of responsibility at the other. Some are tempted to look for a scapegoat in this fallen world, upon whom the blame for this crisis and deaths can be loaded. "Mankind, in the darkness, sat awake thinking that it heard noises and guessing where they came from. Mysterious powers, good, evil, or indifferent, but mostly evil, were felt to be everywhere present, everywhere capable of exercising an influence on man's life." Yet amid all this gloom and darkness and haunted by the fear of death, I believe some still choose to hold on to hope and the faith that something lay beyond our graves.

April 8

Some of my friends have thought about the reason for the present crisis and relate it to our environment's destruction. As Christian, in the middle of this Holy Week, I am reminded that in a way we are like trees. I am grateful that our parents have planted us and given us a good and solid foundation. It is now up to us how to grow. + There was a tree behind our house at Caulfield Ridge that I observed when I looked out at the 18th fairway. It had stood the test of gale-force wind of the seasons when many trees had fallen in Stanley Park. Some of you have read my blog: - http://www.freepilgrim.com/a-continuing-journey-of-belief-and-faith/ ... and not just given it a cursory glance. At least one of you had given me feedback which I appreciated. I have reworded the paragraph on "Gifts and Extended Adolescence" to avoid misinterpretation of my thoughts. I hope that readers do not take umbrage. Instead, I hope readers will delve deeper spiritually. When a tree's roots go deeper into the ground, it becomes more stable and resilient to withstand the environment's elements and forces.

April 10

Today is Good Friday, even for those of us who have not yet embraced the Christian faith. Why is the worst day in human history called good? Because now the worst sinners in human history can be called Forgiven...

April 11

Have we lost our sense of purpose during this crisis? Do we find our-selves useless? Do something good for others. Contribute to the world. Do we have fear? Have we lost hope? If all hope seems lost, reach out to someone you know who cares about you. Darkness and this crisis is only a passing phase. Easter is here for Christians and all. Light is coming. If all hope seems lost, reach out to someone you know who cares about you. Call a friend, a member of our family, your clergy... Faith over fear "Fear thou not; for I am with thee: be not dismayed; for I am thy God: I will strengthen thee; yea, I will help thee; yea, I will uphold thee with the right hand of my righteousness." Isaiah 41:10.

"Jesus said unto her, I am the resurrection, and the life: he that believeth in me, though he were dead, yet shall he live: And whosoever liveth and believeth in me shall never die. Believest thou this?" John 11:25-26 (KJV)

April 16

We look outside, and what do we see that makes us smile? Whatever it is we describe, it has always been there waiting for us to see and appreciate. Perhaps the purpose of this quarantine period is to create a space for us, in the middle of the many responsibilities on this life-long journey, to appreciate what has always been there –the presence of God!

April 17

Whereas before this global crisis, there was a discordant cacophony of voices, now there is a clear, loud message being communicated to all who hear it. Ever since Biblical time, "God whispers to us in our pleasures, speaks in our conscience but shouts in our pain." Millions in the world are listening at this very moment and are walking His Way

April 22

I am aware that it is extremely easy for me to live a quiet life among these bricks of solitude...I am one of the first to self-quarantine (starting March 8th). Leaders have good intentions in laying out their guidelines for isolation. However, I believe our fear does not arise from the pandemic- the fear of the virus dynamics and our unpredictable and unknown response! This fear emerges within our souls, and perhaps the contagion fear is also heightened and transmitted through irresponsible social media and the press?

April 24

At the dawn of this third (3rd) millennium, we woke up to an amazing realization that problems of a disease such as one caused by the novel coronavirus SARS-CoV-2 can be solved entirely. To humanity, in this modern and progressive era, plague is no longer an incomprehensible and uncontrollable force of nature. God can be taken out of the equation. Science and not discernment/prudence (the gift/guiding intellectual skill) will determine how long we will be hunkered down and how we will move forward … "Stay safe" remains a feeble dream of the enervated and shallow-minded …

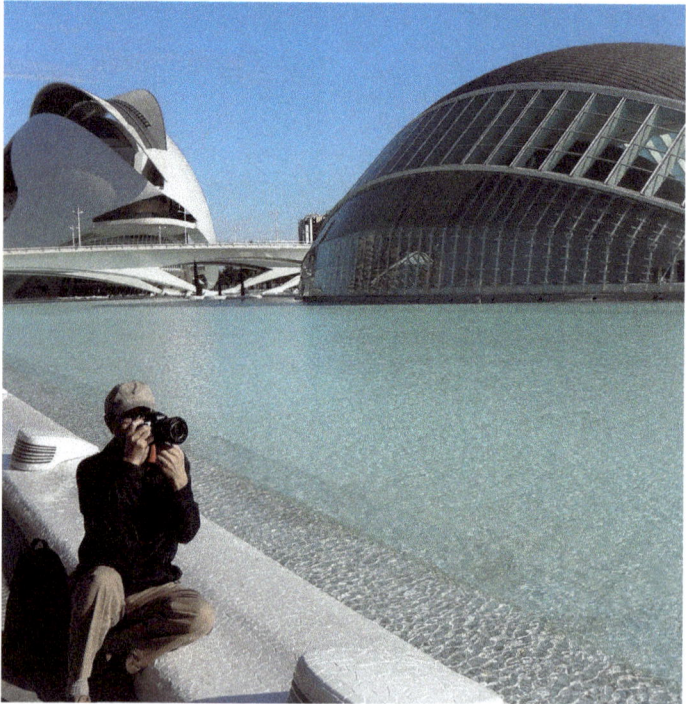

April 27

"And the light shineth in the darkness, and the darkness comprehended it not"- John 1:5 (KJV)

Hastings street Vancouver at 8 am. Ghost town? Why? The fear is in the deep of our soul, not because of COVID-19.

April 28

We are living on a double-edged sword. Are we really protecting the health (physical and spiritual) of our citizens by this prolonged lockdown? I cannot witness (because of my "lock-in"). Still, I believe there are rising rates of domestic violence, drug and alcohol abuse, drug overdose. I hear sirens from emergency vehicles), more pornography use, virtual abuse over the internet, social media bullying, depressions, and suicides (some due to financial ruins caused by shutdowns). So far, the media are not labeling these deaths caused as "deaths caused by the shutdown." Every day we read story after story of coronavirus deaths and hospitals under stress.

All these reports are true, but they do not give us a full picture of reality. If we can see, hear, and read more stories about the shutdown's effects on people's lives as listed above, our views (and our fears) might be more balanced. Those who govern and make decisions during this crisis are honourable people who are doing their best. However, they have not noticed the enormous implications arising out of some of their decisions. Thousands of the elderly do not receive proper care because clinics are closed, and geriatric nurses are laid off. A daughter going to the hospital to visit her mother was not allowed to see her. The mother may soon die, not from the coronavirus but some flu. This is tragic- because she would die alone without seeing her daughter. Have you noticed that there are strict guidelines but no provision even for those who might wish to go to a place of worship? This merits reflection!

April 30

How is self-isolation doing for most of us? Perhaps this "monastic regimen" is not an end in itself, but its end is the health for the soul. This is probably what the monastic way of life, as a regimen, aims at. May we use this given time (or part of it) to ask for revelation of what is unseen - that way, we lack nothing but have the abundance of every gift.

May 1

Today's world view: "When the whole world is running towards a cliff, he who is running in the opposite direction appears to have lost his mind."

May 2

"And if any man think that he knoweth any thing, he knoweth nothing yet as he ought to know." - 1 Corinthians 8:2 (KJV). If we list the issues we are against, the pencil will run out of lead. But if we ask ourselves to document what we are for, the pencil would not have to be re-sharpened!

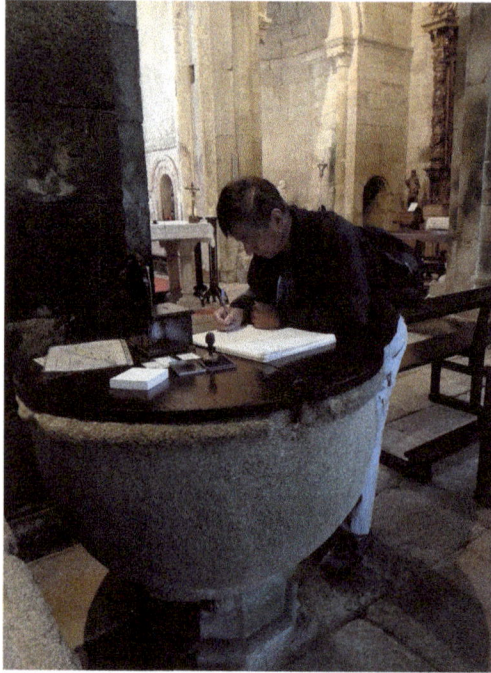

May 4

We choose the "news" instead of the Good News (Evangelion). We tend to act like sheep, following and listening to media outlets and accept all that they present, when we should be listening to the good Sheppard's voice. (John 10:27, KJV)

May 5

Has the virus essentially changed anything important to us? Changed the way we think? Transformed us may be? It has certainly rendered all our "wisdom" obsolete. We know a little more than we knew before, but the unpredictability and fragility of life are still in the thoughts of many as we wrap our minds about it. With all the advances in technology, scientific and medical knowledge in more than a hundred years since the Spanish Flu, we still cannot prevent its occurrence. We learned that to wear masks, wash our hands, and do "social-distancing" in mitigation. Technology and social media can be both a blessing and a curse but, if used wisely, can reduce the stress of isolation. For some (me included), they have brought an awareness that the church's sacramental life continues…

May 6

When is the right time? Do not get me wrong. As a Canadian, I was one of the first to self-quarantine (starting March 8th). We are concerned for the vulnerable. The question now is whether we are still whipping ourselves into a frenzy over COVID-19. Canadians are "nice" people. They do not question. But some think "stay safe" is only for the enervated and shallow-minded. The decision of whether to open for business is not a binary one. If the lockdown continues unwisely, the skeptical voices of those who questioned the lockdown will become more prominent.

This situation may even explode when the chicken comes back to roost. People finally emerge from what many see as an extended vacation period from work and find themselves unemployed, without income, bankrupt and destitute. This will amplify the economic devastation of our country when it is already in bad shape. We have already been informed that increasing debt and budget deficits have become

severe fiscal challenges facing the federal and provincial governments. The combined federal and provincial nominal net debt since
2007/2008 has grown from $837.00 billion to a projected $1.5 trillion
in 2019/20. The combined federal and provincial net debt for 2019//20
is expected to equal 64.3% of the Canadian economy or $39,483 for
every Canadian…and those projections were before this crisis…

May 7

COVID-19 has brought out the best and the worst of us. Very few
have any influence on policy. We believe power is sometimes abused,
and sometimes it is! This makes us frustrated, angry, and hate those
in power. There are right ways and wrong ways to respond. Some of
us do not act constructively in response. It is moving in a destructive

direction, taking the form of anger and attack on one another. It is corrosive to social and family relations… "It is to one's honour to avoid strife, but every fool is quick to quarrel."

May 8

We are the salt of the earth. But if the salt loses its saltiness, how can it be made salty again? It is no longer good for anything except to be thrown out and trampled underfoot. Salt is made up of both sodium and chloride. By itself, sodium is bad for us, so is chloride. Put them together, and we have table salt. Salt flavors the food we eat, and a certain amount of salt is necessary for health and life. During this crisis, as a Christian, I am delighted to hear that what we do is "for the good" of the community, or the greater good, or the good of all…But here we are, quoting only a portion of one of the most quoted verses in the New Testament! When we say these words, we are reminded to refer to Roman 8:28 (KJV) "And we know that all things work together for good to them that love God, to them who are the called according to his purpose." May this be so …

May 9

As I sit here and living this life by the bricks of solitude, my mind drifted to the quiet countryside on the way to Navarrete with my back "supported" by the 7.5 kilos of my rucksack…fantasizing with so many contrasting sensations: the bustles of the cities of Pamplona and Logrono, the calm of so many idyllic Spanish villages, the warmth of the sun, the cool of the early mornings, the warbling sounds of the mating barn sparrows, the fragrance of the wild flowers, the wine at the fountain of Irache and the taste of low sugar and high acid levels of the early grapes from the vineyards we passed…and what the invisible eyes see beyond space and time on this peaceful Path. The other Path is full of annoyance, hate, distractions, distortions of facts and truth which we see in the real world…Which world we want to see is our choice…

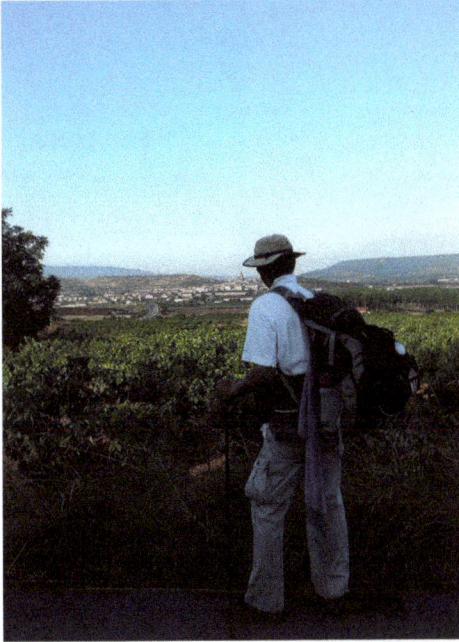

May 10

Today is Mother's Day. We celebrate all mothers, those here, those gone before us, those soon to be...for showing us the direction and the example of AGAPE.

Mother's Day... "Her children arise up, and call her blessed; her husband also, and he praiseth her." Proverb 31:28.

May 11

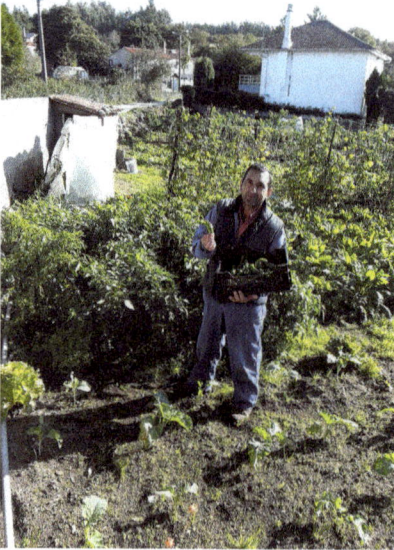

Many people have questions about when everything will return to normal. What is normal? Do we want the normal? Considering our current situation, most of us would like to know the future. COVID-19 will not dramatically alter our society for the better, even though it might change us personally in some ways we may not even be thinking about. We will probably be washing our hands more often from now on. But have we used this season in lockdown to ponder over the effect of what we do? The truth of the matter is that the future is indeed before us. What we choose to do today will ultimately shape our tomorrow. We do not need to predict it. Ask any farmer. He knows if he plants chili, he will harvest chili, not cucumber.

May 12

I believe all can agree that it is possible to criticize the system and circumstance under which we are governed while simultaneously bearing in mind the fallen man's intention and the depravity of the human heart! Swallow our arrogance and pride in acknowledging that the world is not quite divided into the good (us) and the damnable (them) and realising that no leader or political system could ever bring heaven on earth. Although I am usually unperturbed at this stage of my life and generally prefer the vision of peace, this critical time does call me to discern the actual situation wisely. In our country, the current situation, and especially in the United States and whether facts and truth are covered up by fake news, twisted by dishonest media to help paint a good picture of people we admired and used to support or still support…I believe "truth will out"…

May B

Many Canadians rejoice with this announcement: "If you have stopped working because of COVID-19, the Canada Emergency Response Benefit (CERB) may provide you with temporary income support. The CERB provides $500 a week for up to 16 weeks". Some Canadians have received double the expected monthly payments from this new CERB, with more benefits on the way for others… As Friedrich Hayek noted: "With the exception of the period of gold standard, practically all governments of history have used their exclusive power to issue money to defraud and plunder the people".

Should episteme (scientific knowledge) or Doxa (common opinion) be the guiding light for reopening the economy? It would be foolish for us to deny the validity of good science. But "No person or even group of persons, no matter how wise, can attain enough information to plan economic activity from on high" -Jayabalan, Kishore. "Inhuman Economics." We should not rely on one form to the exclusion of other (equally important form) to decide whether to ease the lockdown and gradually open up the economy. This is not a binary decision. I am delighted to learn that the British Columbia Centre for Disease Control ("BCCDC") is taking the BC COVID-19 survey and stating (with humility): "The unintended impacts on the social, economic, physical health, mental wellness and resiliency of communities are not well understood. The BC Centre for Disease Control ("BCCDC"), a part of the Provincial Health Services Authority, wants to understand the impacts of COVID-19 for all BC residents, and to plan the approach for future public health measures". We are grateful for having our health experts in this crisis. However, it is crucial to keep "clear water" between science on the one hand and policy response on the other. Risk assessment should indeed be separated from risk management. Many of us have already long wished that we should just "tap" their expertise but not to put them on "top" as I cited Winston Churchill's refrain that scientific advisors should be "on tap, not on top"…

May 14

To hold persons in power accountable, it is important to distinguish between legal and political accountability. It remains necessary to pay attention to a certain definitive issue concerning the case of lieutenant general Flynn. Priority one accords to a different form of accountability depends on the underlying account to which one is committed. Using the conventional or classical approach, the first item for us to consider is the legal accountability in this case. The political accountability will follow eventually and will be manifested at the ballot box.

At this juncture, one thing is certain. To General Flynn's supporters, the prosecutorial reversal rectified entrapment by the investigators, and true justice is served. To the detractors, it is a politically charged move that represents a further erosion of the rule of law. "rule of law is at risk" in America? At this, I surmise that most first-year Constitutional Law students must be thinking that professor A.V. Dicey is now turning in his grave

May 15

"What is truth?" asked Pontius Pilate. Had Pontius Pilate become desirous to be acquainted with the truth? Is truth a relative concept as our souls find it? Is truth, which is timeless and irrespective of cultural circumstances, binding over us, or does changing culture judge and authorize us to "change" truth in light of "the signs of the times"? Ask a question. Do not just swallow it. Spit it out if it does not taste good!

May 16

The "fear of contagion" continues to trump everything else for us as British Columbia prepares to enter the second phase of its economic reopening plan. *"Death was before their eyes, and everybody began to think of their grave…"*.

A well-researched historical account, "A Journal of the Plague Year" by Daniel Defoe (author of Robinson Crusoe), strangely relates to us of the authorities' measures during the London Plague of 1665-66; measures which resembled those advocated by our health experts. The MDs of the 17th century were ignorant of modern microbiology and epidemiology, but they were just as intense and ferocious about isolation or "social distancing" as we know today. The measures were indiscriminate, not voluntary but coercive. *"I am speaking now of people made desperate by the apprehensions of their being shut up, and their breaking out by stratagem or force, either before or after they were shut up, whose misery was not lessen when they were out, but sadly increased"*. They saw (as we see in our time) cities and towns transformed with streets suspiciously empty… *"It may, however, be added, that the College of Physicians were daily publishing several preparations, which they had considered of in the process of their practice, and which, being to be had in print, I avoid repeating for that reason*"... In our time, Coronavirus briefs are narrated daily through modern media of communications by politicians and health officials to the point of exhaustion.

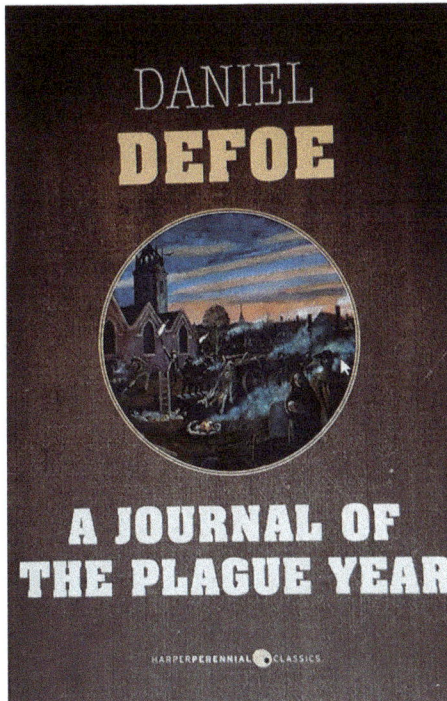

May 18

"SHOW ME YOUR WALK"! For more than two months, we have been hidden, confined our journeys to the trivial ones necessary to get from the bedroom to the kitchen to the study...and only occasional exposures (with sporadic enthusiasm) in the local scenes... Some are beginning to show their "walk" on the "talk" of re-opening the economy...

May 19

Millennials and Generation Z will likely be the ones who will bear the greatest financial brunt of this COVID-19 lockdown. Perhaps (hopefully not) for years to come. Many millennials entered the workforce, which had just recovered from the 2008 financial crisis. Now they are being hammered by this pandemic. Some say the economy will bounce back, but many people are still "fearful." Businesses and the economy are not geared to social distancing. Millions of jobs (particularly related to the hospitality and entertainment industries) are lost, even though some new enterprises may spring up. The development of new non-standard "work" may change the very concept of (traditional) work as we understand it and, accordingly, employment relationships. Yet, motivated by love, we need to nurture and teach (the young) resilience. We will not have "snowflake generations" coming after us…

First of all, we need to "break out" not only from our lockdown (cautiously and safely) but also from the negative thought cycles (robustly and resolutely). We need to stop the dramatization of the COVID-19 situation. It is imperative to push back against catastrophizing and look for/to the upsides. Do not allow some media (however good their intention may be) to sow the seed of discouragement! I remember fondly, when I was attending a banking program at Harvard many years ago, the first thing the professor said was: "Every problem creates an opportunity!"…It is not trite to say that even if opportunity knocks, we still have to get up from our beds (like I just did) and open the door!

May 20

In this season, on my calendar since retirement, I would normally be peregrinating on some foreign soil, widening my horizon, and immersing myself in a different culture. But here I am, voluntarily holed up and surrounded only by good books (prints and Kindle) and old bricks of solitude.

Although as a chorister from young, by nature understand the power of certain pleasant sound arrangements that enthrall me and bewitch my mind, I have often wished I knew something more in musicology and could play the Yamaha piano which is maintaining its presence before me in desperate silence.

In this chosen confinement, at this point in my blessed life, I can only journey back in time and take myself into those sunny "POETS" days (I don't mean "Piss off early, tomorrow's Saturday") of my early years; free to wander down the long-ignored memory lane which I have not taken for more than half a century…

> A thousand flowers, each seeming one
> That learnt by gazing on the sun
> To counterfeit his shining;
> Within whose leaves the holy dew
> That falls from heaven has won anew
> A glory, in declining. : - Elizabeth Barrette Browning

May 21

Is SAR-CoV-2 going to be completely exhausted and the fatal malady spent? Will we find a vaccine, new medicine, or discover any cure? How did it come by? Where specifically it originated? We just do not know. Let the people search for reasons or answers in nature because scientists are unable to. The prevailing view (whether right or not) is that the virus will almost certainly return with a vengeance, perhaps in the Autumn (our autumn?) or sometime in the future. Epidemiologists also predict (judging from the history of viral happenings or occurrences) that there will be a new epidemic every 5 years… "And if any man think that he knoweth any thing, he knoweth nothing yet as he ought to know."

We have learned that very plague, from the plagues in Egypt as told in Exodus, The Justinian Plagues pandemic (542-546), The Black Death pandemic (1347 to 1351), The Italian Plague epidemic of 1629-1631, The Great Plague of London epidemic (1665 to 1666), The Bubonic Plague pandemic that began in Yunnan 1855 all the way down in human history to the Spanish Flu pandemic H1N1 (1918-1919) just somehow petered out. **"…we've seen them just peter out and we don't understand this petering out. Despite the very sophisticated computer mathematical models we have seen, we just don't know what is going to happen"**… But we will give thanks for the diseases to abate one way or the other and sing His praise, and we will not be like the children of Israel, who looked back, saw the Egyptians overwhelmed at the Red Sea, and soon forgot the work of His Mighty Hand…

May 22

Experts have clashed over research into the efficacy of wearing masks (even homemade face coverings) in public. There is no question that public health experts have at times given confusing guidance on mask-wearing. The authorities were aware that as the COVID-19 outbreak continued to spread and expand globally, the supply chain for these devices would be stressed if demand exceeded available supplies. But what about it now? Has the attitude about face mask changed and become too politicized? It seems face mask has now become a political football in the age of COVID-19. Despite the controversy, May continues to make them and it is a good thing!

As the economy opens up, and more of us are heading out into public spaces, we need to avoid using or viewing it (the face mask) as a political symbol. Wearing a face mask does not mean one is blindly submitting to the orders of the authorities or that wearing one is a sign of compassion/that we are good people (just because health experts now say cloth face masks protect others from disease transmission if the wearer has the virus but is asymptomatic). May we make the choice that we feel comfortable with…

May 23

What is risk? Re-opening carries continued risks. Uncertainty is at its heart. We are unsure whether COVID-19 will likely spike. Also, we may be uncertain what its consequences would be if it did occur. We are fearful of a second wave. We are provided with many guidelines- "All employers must work with their employees to develop their safety plan to protect everyone as they prepare to reopen." But "rules-based risk management" will not diminish either the likelihood or the impact of a disaster... *Managing Risks: A New Framework - Harvard Business Review.* https://hbr.org/2012/06/managing-risks-a-new-framework. Whether we are consciously aware of it or not, we are actually doing risk management all the time. Riding a bike down the mountain is risky. When we leave the relatively risk-free surrounding of our home and cross the street is a risk. Walking on a deserted street on foreign soil is a risk. We watch and manage our risks naturally. I confess that I had never really and seriously thought about (or of the difference between) risk assessment and risk management until the day I attended a program at INSEAD Fontainebleau. With humility, I recall the professor came in and said: "Today we will talk about Risk Assessment and Risk Management!". Many knew risk ASSESSMENT in banking, yet it had not prevented many financial institutions' failure in the 2007-2008 financial crisis.

In our present health situation, instead of "fearing fear itself" we need to consider the causes of the problem we might (ourselves) personally be facing. The source and the overall risk that we have assessed should not be ignored. It is foolish to do so. However, because COVID-19 is not even a national problem but a global one, all we can effectively address is the one affecting us and our "neighbours" in our circumstance and at our (micro) level. Should I wear a mask? Have I washed my hands? Remember that it is not possible to eliminate all risks... so we pray and hope that we be given the spirit not of fear but of power and love and self-control to manage...

May 25

Children are returning to schools… Education seems to develop us "properly" so we can deal with and manage our daily life activities in the best possible ways, socially and economically. However, much more than knowledge of facts and skills are required of us to live fully as we journey through this life! Can we find the tool for building a society that can think critically and creatively through unpredictable challenges across different disciplines, including disciplines to unfold the specific content of faith and ethics?

Our children are facing some of human history's most significant challenges. The world is becoming borderless, increasingly dynamic, and complex. Education is the vehicle for ensuring that generations to come will navigate this complexity, open the human minds with thorough understanding, enhance our collaborations in areas of common interests, and help problem-solving across cultures. Education certainly has the power to do all these, and much more, to change lives. But more importantly, does it make us do what is good, do justice, love kindness, and walk humbly? Does education give us purpose and make us dutiful? to perform the duties expected and required of us?...

May 26

We are not dinosaurs. We are aware that progress is a good thing and we are grateful for it. In this time of partial lockdown, we still can "socialise" with zoom and Google Meet etc... But even though social media appears to have built a "semblance of community" the relationship is lacking depth. Who is the "person" in our Facebook friend?

Smart phones are causing a "frayed" relationship. Sociologists say we are living in an age of "networked individualism." This leads to distraction that ends up undermining the benefits of social interaction. We have lost our innate ability to listen to others and see things around us. It is not trite to say that progress, unfortunately, is not all gain. With progress and technological advances, human behaviours and relationships are undergoing fundamental changes, and it is not all good...We are also so "woke" that (as we chill) decorum, good manner and etiquette, social relations, and the way we talk would have already been in museums if they were tangible and solid things... A Dominican Friar once noted: "the most technologically advanced countries face the humilities of their limits"...

May 27

Ascension (last Sunday) and Pentecost (coming Sunday) are two events of great salvific and historical importance to Christians around the world and are commemorated in this season of the year. From Pentecost on, the Holy Spirit would come to live in everyone who repents and believes in Christ. "I will not leave you comfortless: I will come to you." -John 14:18 (KJV). The Holy Spirit not only makes us aware of our needs; It empowers us to walk with Christ and puts us into the right relationship with Him and with one another. Although the Gospel (Evangelion) is inherently personal, it is not merely (and neither meant to be) a private affair. Then he told them, "And he said unto them, Go ye into all the world, and preach the gospel to every creature…" - Mark 16:15. Imbued with the "glad tidings" of new life in Jesus Christ, Christians fanned out from Jerusalem, Judea, and Samaria to carry this Gospel into every nook and cranny of the Roman Empire, to faraway lands, to Ethiopia and India and into all the world…and continue to do…

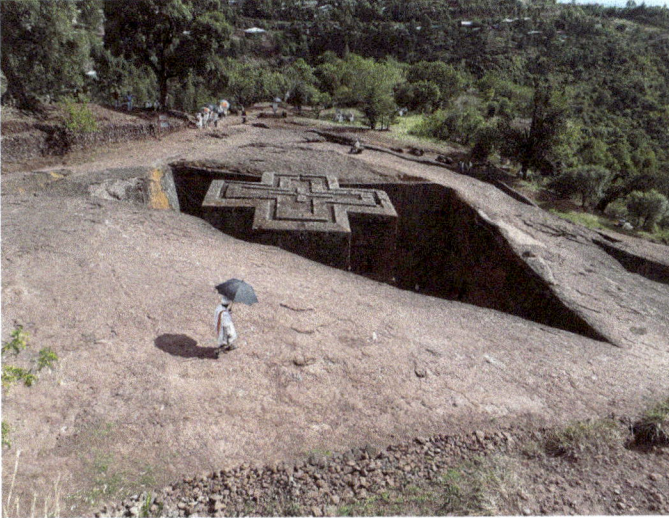

May 30

Does snatching the excuse by one individual that a person is outside the law's protection and then torture him justify a society to turn itself into society without law and order? Resulting in having a society function (if at all) without a more responsive governance system to protect citizens from criminality? What we are witnessing is clearly violence and destruction, not only in the pragmatic world but in (the world without) ethics as well…An evil thought that brings man conscious only of himself and that God, the state, and society does not exist?

June 1
at 6:25 am

The **Decalogue**- the list of ethical principles in **Exodus 20**:1–17…
God gave the **Ten Commandments** to us because he wants us to live
a good life - a peaceful, joyful, and productive life. Abandon any of
them; the alternative is chaos…Do we then (want to) overthrow these
Laws? By no means!

On the contrary, we try upholding them. These Laws do not call for
meritorious works but obedience which flows from our faith. Political
correctness has made it a sad day for society (as we witness the chaos
in recent times) when our law's moral foundation and the acknowl-
edgment of God have been hidden from us…

June 2

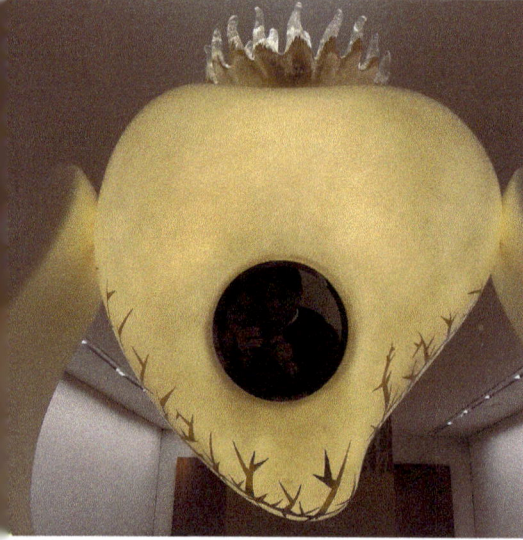

What is "Love"? C.S Lewis talked about the "Four Loves":

Storge (empathy "love"), Philia (friend "love"), Eros (romantic "love"), and Agape (unconditional "God love"). Often, in the modern "liberal" era and evolutionary theology, we misinterpret what "love" is… To disprove our misunderstanding of the word "love" in Christianity, it is instructive for us to study the Gospel of John 2:13-22 when Jesus (made a scourge of small cords) drove the corrupt and venal out of the temple.

John 8:31-59 dovetails with John 2:13-22. These Scriptures disprove any myths that Jesus was soft on what he saw and considered "wrong" (sin). Jesus loves the "person" but not the "wrong" (sin) of the person. In the exchange with the Pharisees, Jesus pulled no punches. Those religious leaders and their followers continued to resist and confronted Jesus. They relied on their arrogance and insults, to which (we learn) Jesus responded with harsh, blunt, and undiluted rebukes!

Should love abrogate discipline and punishment? We are all accountable for our actions! In hoping to bring children up "properly," my paternal grandmother (of old) used to say in Hakka: "Ngai mah ngee yin vui ngai syak ngee; I darr ngee yin vui ngai oi ngee (I scold you because I care for you; I punish you because I love you)"… "我责骂你是因为我在乎你;我惩罚你是因为我爱你"!

40

June 3

"Once you learn to read, you will be forever free.": - Frederick Douglass. We are informed that Douglas was born into slavery around 1817, and like many slaves, the exact date of his birth was unknown. As a young slave, he became interested in literacy, read, and copied Bible verses ("Life and Times of Frederick Douglass"). He escaped from slavery and became a national leader and one of the most famous intellectuals of his time.

Regardless of how many diplomas, degrees, and certifications we have, we can always learn more by reading. All eminent men were voracious readers and the "greats" in history and in our time know that the best knowledge is waiting inside a book (e-book). But we are what we read, and the truth is that, if we do it right, our education never ends, our horizon appropriately widened, and we become more insightful. We think differently. We learn to break the constraints of our assumptions, past "knowledge", predispositions, and more importantly, "bias." This thinking mode goes by other names, such as lateral thinking or "thinking outside the box."

Someone once asked a prolific reader: "What is your favourite book?" but the most popular book in the world, the Bible, was not on his list. **As long as we have faith in our cause and an unconquerable willpower, salvation will not be denied us."** : -Winston Churchill's address to the Congress of the United States on December 26, 1941. I am left wondering what great works fed into the mind of Churchill to influence his philosophy.

Although it is impossible to obtain exact figures, the Bible Society's survey concluded that around 2.5 billion copies were printed between 1815 and 1975. According to Guinness World Records, as of 15 March 2015, the Bible is the best-selling book of all time, with an estimated 5 billion copies sold and distributed. The whole Bible had been translated into 349 languages.

June 4

In all or any form (and to various degrees), racism has been a plague on humanity. This should not be for Christians. We must deal with this ongoing issue of racism and prejudice, which is a spiritual virus. But how? He who practises racism should seek repentance.

On the other hand, Christians (who are victims) need to learn to forgive as we ask the Father for forgiveness. But instead, some of us Christians are encouraging and partaking in chaos and lawlessness! Keeping in mind the Scripture (John 2:13-16), what would Jesus do if people try to burn down His House?

This week Christians around the world celebrate the Trinity (the three Persons of God). The Trinity is a term employed to signify the central doctrine of Christianity- the truth that in the unity of the Godhead, there are Three Persons: the Father, the Son, and the Holy Spirit. As Christians, we are taught by Jesus to recognize Him as the eternal son of God. When His ministry was drawing to a close, Jesus promised his disciples that the Father would send another Divine

Person, the Spirit (Pentecost), in His place. Finally, before ascension, He revealed this doctrine in explicit terms, bidding the disciples: "Go ye therefore, and teach all nations, baptizing them in the name of the Father, and of the Son, and of the Holy Ghost":-Matthew 28:19 (KJV)... "Let voices rise and interweave, by hope and love set free, to shape in song this joy, this life: the dance of Trinity!": - Richard Leach.

June 5

"Amazing Grace" is one of our best-loved and best-known hymns. It was written by John Newton, a slave trader who became an abolitionist. During a slave trade voyage in 1748, the ship (*Greyhound*) John Newton on was caught in a horrendous storm. Newton prayed to God and the vessel drifted to safety. He took this as a sign from the Almighty and marked it as his conversion to Christianity. "I cannot consider myself to have been a believer in the full sense of the word, until a considerable time afterwards," he later wrote. However, we learn that he did begin reading the Bible and began to view his captives (slaves) with more sympathy and empathy. He had probably realized and thought much as Frederick Douglass (who came later) did… "The first work of slavery is to mar and deface those character-istics of its victims which distinguish *men* from *things* and *person* from *property*," and 'Its first aim is to destroy all sense of high moral and religious responsibility." (My Bondage and My Freedom): - Frederick Douglass …

Newton did not write the music. Musicologists believe the tune to "Amazing Grace is Scottish or Irish because it sounds good on the bagpipes (the other is "Scotland the Brave"). Yet some believe that the melody was probably a folk tune from the plantations of the American South… Perhaps what everyone can agree on is that it has been recorded more than any other hymns in the world. The hymn, which relates and describes profound religious elation, is estimated to be performed more than 10 million times annually and has appeared on over 11,000 albums.

June 6

"I want to teach people that liberty does not consist in having your house robbed by organized gangs of thieves, and in leaving the principal streets of London in the nightly possession of drunken women and vagabonds." said Sir Robert Peel the British Home Minister almost two hundred ago...The concept of modern policing (a professional law enforcement corps) had its roots in the establishment of the Metropolitan Police Act of 1829. The only weapon for the police was the truncheon.

The "Bobbies" were friends of the citizenry in those early days of mine in England. They were also my (never needed) "protectors" even amid a youth-driven cultural revolution that was taking place, and the truncheon was still their only weapons in the swinging sixties. The "Bobbies" were also my "Tourist guides" as I explored England as a young law student...The "Bobby and me" relationship was enduring, comforting, reassuring. These days we find ourselves, too often, clawing on the word "cops". What has changed? Have we changed? Has society changed?

When social historians look back in the future, they would be constrained to note that we have had the most numbers of (some consider senseless and purposeless) protests and demonstrations over the last 50 years. Why and how have we arrived at these chaotic moments, with malignant civil unrests at this point in time in our lives? Liberty should probably arrive to face the demarcation line of its limit. We understand that simplifying the underlying causes may lead us to the wrong solutions, but criminality and violence cannot be and should not be condoned or excused. Are we really "woke"? Reverend Martin Luther King Jr. had a dream. A good dream! But his dream remains an unfulfilled dream when the "Prince of Peace" is hidden from us, hidden from children in schools and political arenas, and as long as man is aware only of his own self, color, race, and consciousness only of his own presence and existence.

June 8
at 6:00 am

"Free association and the ability to meet in the public square is a fundamental right," Premier John Horgan of British Columbia said. He is correct under the Canadian Constitution Acts 1867-1982. Although quoting "Freedom of Assembly" under Section 2(c) is more appropriate even though section 2(c) of the Charter has received only limited judicial interpretation. In practice even if submissions on section 2(c) are made, courts tend to resolve the issues under section 2(b): - Figueres v. Toronto (City) Police Services Board, 2015 ONCA 208) …However, is this secular "freedom" really fundamental? Is this individual secular "freedom" (distinguished from "freedom" of the gospels) for the common good?

On the subject of "Assembly", is it true that our emotion works hand-in-hand with our cognitive process (or the way we think) about an issue or situation? In the recent George Floyd protests, we witness that emotion plays a major role in influencing society and perhaps even attitude change. Emotions play out in cities, states, and countries around the world outside Minneapolis, where George Floyd, a black man, died after a white police officer Derek Chauvin knelt on his neck (a horrendous act no decent man should allow). We have noted that emotional appeal is commonly found in advertisings (such as cigarette ads we see on T.V.). Emotional appeal is also found in political messages. "Systemic Racism", "Black Lives Matter" are examples of these political messages. These are persuasive messages and are very convincing, not only to Asians and Black minorities but also to some others who may internalise the stigma directed towards them, blaming and devaluing themselves (the "white guilt" of victimizing Blacks) …

With hope of widening my horizon on "victimization," I found it interesting and instructive to study Shelby Steele's thinking as a black conservative. Shelby Steele is of the view that Blacks and Whites together have in recent times destroyed the promise of the Civil Rights era. Steele believes that the use of victimization is the greatest hindrance for black Americans. In his view, white Americans see Blacks as victims to ease their guilty conscience, and Blacks attempt to turn their status as victims into a kind of currency that will purchase nothing of real or lasting value. He contends that Blacks have been twice betrayed: "first by slavery and oppression and then by group preferences mandated by the government, which discourage self-agency and personal responsibility in Blacks".

June 9

Social media has "erased" physical distances and "dissolved" geographical limitations. George Floyd's death, which fuelled protests across North America, instantly ignited reaction across Asia, even from unassuming persons sitting in humble coffee shops out in small towns in my native country. By human nature, political protest against injustice is selective. Because of this choice, George Floyd has overshadowed the protest in Hong Kong, which is much closer geographically to Malaysia than Minneapolis. The idea of a political system based on "limited democracy" seems to be no longer an important factor or issue to be considered in contemporary politics.

Not so long ago, when COVID-19 surfaced, we heard so many inspiring stories of people coming together; choirs sang in harmony around the world. People and communities were kind to each other, with strangers helping the aged and vulnerable. The "colourless" glues for the common good which bound us together just suddenly vanished into thin air, and the "dark" gods appear in their place. Have we found new meaning and purpose in life? We worship the god of identity politics and pursue lawlessness and mayhem! COVID-19 may come to an end, but will the "dark" gods let us live in peace?

June 10

Thomas Merton (the trappiest monk) once noted: "Geographic pilgrimage is the symbolic acting out of an inner journey. The inner journey is the interpolation of the meanings and signs of the outer pilgrimage. One can have one without the other. It is best to have both"… This pilgrimage on the Camino de Santiago (outer and inner journey) took me beyond my own physical self and beyond the consciousness of my own presence and existence. But how can I explain? That yet, I came to the end of this long journey and saw that the stranger I met was no other than myself…with the realization that I had recently fallen when I preferred to remember only the ills of some but chose to inter the good of so many others with their bones!

People of faith are facing growing persecution around the world, fuelled mainly by religious extremism and repressive governments. Where are the protesters against "religio-ethnic cleansing when the Pope warned of "genocide? Not intended to make light of the morally reprehensible treatment of George Floyd, the "dark" gods are urging us to see and remember **only** the ill of one bad police officer (may God forgive him). On the other hand, they tell us to forget, ignore, disregard, and be ungrateful for the good of so many who are still serving us!

"Yet a little while is the Light with you. Walk while ye have the Light, lest darkness come upon you; for he, that walketh in darkness knoweth not whither he goeth." John 12:35 (KJV)

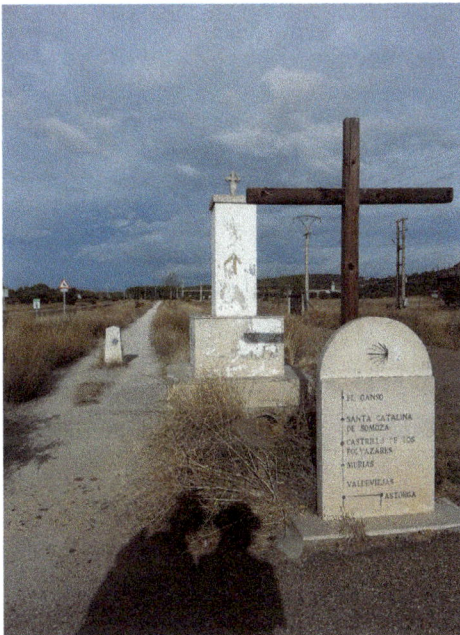

June 11

Have we failed to carry out our primary mission to treat the patients and help to transform lives?

Many are in concert with those showing signs and shouting: "Black Lives Matter", "Systemic Racism" Mr. Prime Minister! Please kneel down with the patients and be sure that they remain completely fixated on these political messages. Fixation on these messages will serve as an excellent distraction from advancing the virtue, character, and the things the patients can control. Make sure the patients are in a constant state of angst, frustration, and general disdain towards the rest of the human race so that they will avoid developing any kind of charity or inner peace.

Most importantly, be sure to keep the patients obsessed. Ensure that they believe the problem is **completely and solely** due to the "broken system" and the others "out there. Yet (from personal experience) I understand how some patients can recuperate by themselves… then there are other stories… "I grew up in a time when there was real systemic racism. I remember as an eighth-grade student I was the only black student and I got the highest academic achievement and the teacher got up and berated the other students. They weren't trying hard enough because a black kid was number one.": - Dr. Ben Carson

June 13

I believe, and I thank God on this beautiful Saturday morning, that I have this heart He has given me to put something meaningful in… Police abandoned the East precinct in the Capitol Hill neighbourhood of Seattle and effectively handed the area to the protesters they had clashed over for days. The armed occupation and "establishment" of the "Capitol Hill Autonomous Zone" were broadcasted on some Networks and live-streamed over the internet. "I Have A Dream…" I couldn't help feeling, deep in my heart, that the dream of Rev. Martin Luther King Jr. has been shattered, black lives betrayed, and the promise of the Civil Rights era destroyed. His legacy encompasses not just meaningful decisions and actions that led to the steadfast development and progressions of humanitarian rights. He stood intending to achieve these rights for all through **nonviolence!**

Life is an ongoing dream…However, the Scripture tells us that it is important what we have in our heart. "But the LORD said to David my father, Forasmuch as it was in thine heart to build an house for my name, thou didst well in that it was in thine heart"- 2 Chronicles 6:8 (KJV)

Many of us in life start out dreaming and building some kind of temple, a temple of character, a temple of justice, a temple of peace. I suppose one of the greatest agonies of life is that we are constantly trying to finish that which unfinishable…Perhaps it is like Franz Schubert's "Unfinished Symphony."

No.8 in B minor…

June B

What some churches are doing... Good policies are needed but can policies by themselves eradicate racism? Has the Church lost sight of its primary mission to transform lives? The church's mission is to transform the lives of both oppressors and the oppressed and to save lost souls. Too many church leaders believe they are reaching a world that no longer exists (they are probably right) and therefore ended up secularly in local and party politics. Jesus suffers injustice, and he forgives. Is the word "forgiveness" found in sermons and homilies over the last 50 years? Have followers of Christ learned to forgive? We will always be in bondage and never free until we have forgiven the wrongs others have done to us!

The new generation of bishops, priests, and pastors seem to preach more than they teach. A good one can do both. I default to teaching. The Bible teaches. We learn from the Holy Scriptures that which we have not experienced or are unable to experience. Preaching facilitate emotions, and people follow (e.g., kneeling down by some church leaders for "Black Lives Matter" and Systemic Racism" is preaching and not teaching). Is salvation something played out in the drama of "Taking The Knee"? "Take, my brethren, the prophets, who have spoken in the name of the Lord, for an example of suffering affliction, and of patience" - James 5:10 (KJV)

June 15

"Information" is not necessary knowledge, as I learned the other day just by watching the "news" (because I was misinformed). We have also been informed that "knowledge is not wisdom." As we "progress," we seem to be engaging ourselves more and more in the modern project of epistemology - being more concerned with "knowing" than "being"… In our noisy and impulsive pursuit of knowledge (e.g., dialer, SMS & notifications on smart phones) we actually produce no useful "fruits"… There are times when we seem to know and are remarkable in our sphere of activity but make little headway. We begin with an idea but never going deeper or even beyond the outer bark of our idea. Some other time we read but soon forget as if we have not read at all.

However, it is worse if we don't try to acquire knowledge - to know the fact. We can gain knowledge by studying history, the past, the experience. It's important also that we recognize our history - the good and the bad and learn from it. What happened, happened. Some people learn from history; others want to erase it from their minds as if it never happened. We learn from the Bible, and it does not tell only rosy stories - "And they made their lives bitter with hard bondage, in mortar, and brick." Exodus 1:14 (KJV). Some of us travel extensively but going nowhere, with horizon no more widened than that of the armchair tourist, and returning home with nothing of value to impart… "If any of you lack wisdom, let him ask of God, that giveth to all men liberally, and upbraideth not; and it shall be given him." James 1:5 (KJV)

Just a thought: Had the Karnak, the statues and reliefs of Ra'amses been destroyed (by the "cancel culture" that we witness today), much of the historical record etched in stone showing that the Israelites were living and working in Goshen and Ra'amses (1876-1446 BC) would have been lost!

June 16

Perhaps we are seeking the wrong solution in dealing with the cause of and the fight against racism. Tragic reactions and devastating fallout from racism continue today. We have been demonstrating and protesting since the Civil Rights Movement. Secular atonement narratives have not been effective. They are not working and never will. The violent resistance to oppression only continues a cycle of violence. We need the Prince of Peace but sadly many churches are adopting the secular way of reparation.

It is far better to let the oppressor's hatred for the sin of racism and the grace and forgiveness of the oppressed to lead us to a new creation (the new "race" of us redeemed). This is our only hope for racial reconciliation. Who shall ascend to the hill of the Lord? Who shall stand in His holy place? "Create in me a clean heart, O God and renew the right spirit in me": - Psalm 51:10 (KJV)

June 17

One of the founding fathers of America, Patrick Henry, was best known for his declaration "Give me liberty or give me death" to the Second Virginia Convention held on March 23, 1775 at St. John's Church in Richmond, Virginia. According to English philosopher and historian Bernard Mayo: " …its expressions seemed to have burned themselves into men's memories. Certainly, its spirit is that of the fiery orator who in 1775 so powerfully influenced Virginians and events leading to American independence."

James Russell in his work "Stanzas on Freedom"

True freedom is to share,
All the chains our brothers wear
And with heart and hand to be
Earnest to make others free.

I read Russell's three times and am wondering to what extent this tells us about true freedom. Can we set others truly free? On our life-long journey, we will encounter difficulties. We will feel hurt. We will feel oppressed, and we then put chains on ourselves. We will not be free until we have forgiven people who have hurt us. So, do we forgive? As it turns out, we all have the freedom of choice, but we are not free from the consequences of our choices. As a Christian, I can understand that we can claim political freedom, but we cannot claim moral freedom because, in reality (even though some of us may deny it) we are bondmen of sin. The freedom proclaimed by Christ is the true freedom for us, for it is the freedom of our true life, delivered from the thraldom of our sin into union with God... That is the real and true freedom no power can restrain... "And ye shall know the truth, and the truth shall make you free."; -John 8:32 (KJV)

June 18

Opening up the economy...some will and can continue to work at home and be productive in their respective fields...However, for other businesses and industries, "Guidelines" for opening up the economy had been unveiled with several phased approaches based on public health experts' advice. These proposed steps help officials to get people back to work, and at the same time continuing to protect lives.

The OECD released its twice-a-year economic outlook on Wednesday, presented two scenarios - one where the coronavirus continues to recede, and another where the second wave of rapid contagion erupts later in 2020. It said the second wave of SARS-CoV-2 is as likely as not. OECD Chief Economist Laurence Boone said both forecasts are equally probable…So, should the "potential" of the 2nd wave of Covid-19 going to deter the rest of us from returning to work?… "if any would not work, neither should he eat"!

"For we hear that there are some which walk among you disorderly, working not at all, but are busybodies." Thessalonians 3:11(KJV).

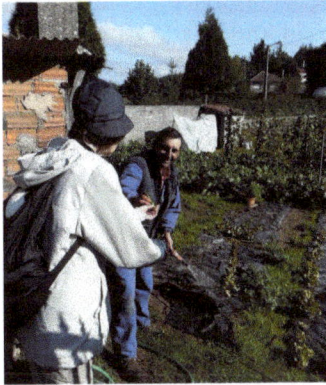

June 20

Understanding slavery, the situation, and the law… It is estimated that there are today over 40 millions (who knows?) people in the world who are subject to slavery: forced labor, sex trade, etc. It is indisputable that modern slavery is practised. There is not enough demonstration, protest, and outcry, certainly not as much publicized around the world as the tragic case of George Floyd. Why? (not intended to make light of the morally reprehensible treatment of George Floyd) but why? Shouldn't we be more concerned with the magnitude and tragedy of modern slavery? This it a sign (of the "sickness" in our society) that we got it all wrong!

And what is the solution to end modern slavery and racism? A person needs to be reformed from the inside out. A person who has accepted the gift of salvation and freedom from the slavery of sin will realize that enslaving another human being is wrong. He will, in turn be gracious towards others. That would be the Bible's prescription for ending slavery and racism. There is no other way to transform people and reform society!

Because the Bible gives instructions on how slaves should be treated (Deuteronomy 15:12-15; Ephesians 6:9; Colossians 4:1) many see this as the Bible condoning all forms of slavery. We fail to understand that slavery in biblical times was very different from the slavery that was practised in the past few centuries in other parts of the world. Most of them were just servants whom Jesus often refers to in his parables (e.g., Luke 15:17-20).

Both the Old and New Testaments condemn the practice of "man-stealing," which happened in Africa in the 16th to 19th centuries. The blacks were hunted, rounded up by slave-hunters, who sold them to slave traders, who brought them to work on plantations and farms in the New World...This practice is abhorrent to God. In fact, the penalty for such a crime in the Mosaic Law was death: "And he that stealeth a man, and selleth him, or if he be found in his hand, he shall surely be put to death.": -Exodus 21:16 (KJV).

June 22

There is Hope … a double whammy has hit us in the last couple of months, the COVID-19 pandemic and the death of George Floyd… followed by the madness of mob protests, chaos, lawlessness, tear gas, toppled statues, and call to defund the police. This double whammy and madness have dashed the hopes of many people. The Greek philosopher Aristotle teaches that virtue is the mean between two vices. "That moral virtue is a mean, then, and in what senses it is so, and that it is a mean between two vices, the one involving **excess**, the other **deficiency…** Hence it is no easy task to be good. For in everything it is not an easy task to find the middle, e.g., to find the middle of a circle is not easy for everyone but for him who knows…Wherefore goodness is both rare and laudable." (W.D. Ross translated this excerpt from Book II of Aristotle's Nicomachean Ethics).

For Christians, "Hope" is a virtue, and we keep returning to this virtue of hope, which is rooted in our trust in God, who will not fail us with His triumphant power. Hope is not false optimism. It does not mean that we do not have difficulties or no setbacks. It does not downplay the challenges we still have to face. Hope is not a delusion even though we feel young and excited and we "fly" when we have hope and that the future is open to us. We look forward to unforeseen opportunities yet to come. The present madness will be gone... Let us keep the words of the prophet Isaiah before our eyes: "But they that wait upon the LORD shall renew their strength; they shall mount up with wings as eagles; they shall run, and not be weary; and they shall walk, and not faint..."- Isaiah 40;31

June 24
at 6:33 am

COVID -19 has been terrorizing us for several months…What is the correct perspective for us to put ourselves into, assuming there is a single correct perspective for us to put into? Most people, I surmise, would veer between panic and complacency. Recent news showing exponential growth in the number of cases (spike or the potential of a second wave) induces a state of anxiety, and then a histogram showing a decline in the number of deaths the day before causes a burst of relief and jubilation that the worst is over. We do not seem to doubt these "facts." Neither the authors of these two scenarios' status is challenged though they are no more in agreement than a Democrat with a Republican or a militant secularist with a theocrat. Besides, (not intended to depreciate our good scientists and health officials). We seem to place great emphasis on persons who wrap themselves in the white coats in the laboratory and continue to make predictions and claim to know the future, with the wildly inconsistent results we see in our current crisis. When a society's culture is inclined to regard mortal's scientific predictions as infallible, we are in deep trouble. It is pertinent to ask ourselves in this increasingly agnostic society (where the foundations of our polities are corrupt and falling into moral decay) what has actually (already) been **revealed** to us and provided us with the right guidance for the future?… When we begin to believe and understand, our cynical laughter will become laughter of joy.

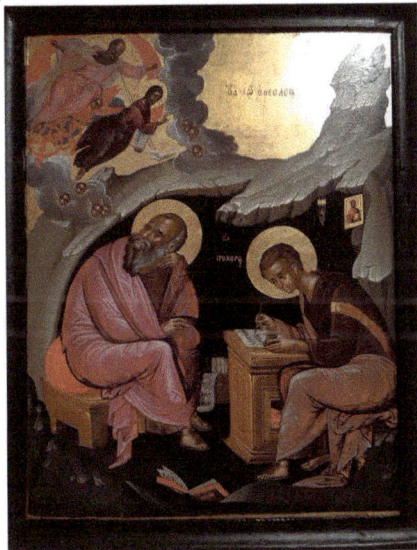

June 25

Most of us trust our carnal minds instead of believing and trusting the Work of God. Our mind set on the flesh refuses to take orders from His Word. We are oblivious that man is constantly being deceived and at the same time mocked. Good and evil are carried out within and determined in the hearts and minds of the mortal man. A voice tells the man: "You are what you are, a self-made man. Be yourself and do whatever you like. You have total freedom to act the way you want. You are the reason for your decision. You can do it because you can." and the man says: "Amen."

We think our ways are always right in our own eyes, in our self-righteousness. It is manifested in all the actions, the chaos, and the lawlessness we witness going on in our society and around us. This is because we have never had a comparison. We need to go through a change (a transformation), an experience, before we can recognize right from wrong, good from evil, truth from falsehood. I will not pretend to know the answer…Just because we do not realize we are in bondage of sin does not change the fact that we are bound. "Let no man deceive himself. If any man among you seemeth to be wise in this world, let him become a fool, that he may be wise." 1 Corinthians 3:18 (KJV).

June 26

The theology of Forgiveness…In 1971 (half a century ago) the General Synod of the Anglican Church of Canada declared June 21st as a "National Indian Day of Prayer" and requested all dioceses to commend this day to parishes and congregations throughout Canada. On July 12th, 2019, The Anglican Church of Canada (in an open letter) offered **"An Apology for Spiritual Harm"** for all Indigenous Peoples. Last Sunday (June 21st, 2020) a Litany for the Healing and

Restoration was recited... Thousands of Canadian Anglicans involved themselves in a ritual act of confession, admitting their guilt (some without racial privilege, no "supremacy" or historical connection). It was guilt by association of sins even if they have never personally committed those sins.

In attempting to find a solution, we seem to be replacing the church's theology of **forgiveness ("forgive us our trespasses as we forgive those who trespass against us...")** with a secular atonement narrative that undermines the Christian narrative. Despite what has been said and done in the name of Jesus, there is no resolution and reconciliation. There will never be peace in and among us until the person "harmed" accept grace and practise the gift of forgiveness. At the end of my pilgrimage on the Camino de Santiago, I realized that I had fallen (in following popular culture) when I preferred to remember only the ills of some but chosen to inter the good of so many with their bones. It is far better for Christians to let their hatred for the sin lead us to a new creation's true narrative (those redeemed in Christ). This is the only hope for reconciliation. The new creation, wrote St. John, is made up "of all nations, and kindreds, and people, and tongues..." (Revelation 7:9).

June 27

The Ancient Greek word "theo" means "god". The word "logy" also comes from Greek, meaning "word". I have been posting much about my "theology", even though nothing that I have posited may have helped a person to grasp what it means to encounter the Living God who loves all of us: - John 3:16 (KJV).

Pythagoras (ca 575 - ca 490 BCE) was probably the first among the ancient philosophers to affirm that the "number governs the forms and the ideas" and that he was the first to use the term "kosmos" for indicating the harmony and symmetry that regulates the universe. What brings social harmony? Three things bring harmony…We only talk about liberty in economics, the politics of equality, but we have forgotten about fraternity…

June 29

The Cross, the Christian religion's principal symbol, recalls the Crucifixion of Jesus Christ and the redeeming benefits and salvation for all mankind. The symbol of the Christian Cross played out in the gospel is symmetrical and harmonious. In fraternity, Christians bear the cross with Jesus. May the Prince of Peace bring "Pacem in Terris." Let us lift up the cross, lift Up the Cross, for it is the total gift of God for us and with us…The Emmaus Journey (on the road to Emmaus) in Luke 24:13-35, one the best sketches of biblical scenes, is a model for a Christian's own journey to a deeper faith and to help others make the journey…

June 30

Covid-19 has given me the "monastic" way of living over the last few months and, in this time of crisis, the opportunity to take on a deeper spiritual journey... Yet, with modern technology, I was brought to an awareness of what goes on outside these brick walls of solitude. This has provided me a window with a clearer view into a larger world of concerns, that our fractured world needs us to think and take the matter a little bit more seriously. That we need to feel about the importance of asking questions to which there may be no easy answers.

Even though my own journey is utterly personal, rooted in the particular circumstances at this stage of my life, perhaps it may have a universal resonance. Why have I given myself so much space on my Facebook Wall to what may seem trivial and irrelevant from some other perspectives? But in a sense, it is my hope that my many postings, since the pandemic lockdown began, may be seen by many (to paraphrase French structural anthropologist Claude Levi-Strauss) as "good to think with"...

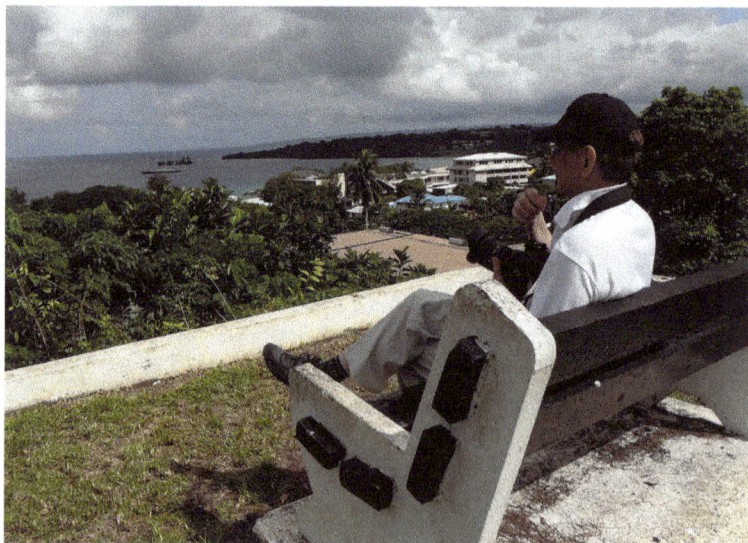

July 1

On Canada Day, I remember the Preamble of The Canadian Charter of Rights & Freedoms: "Whereas Canada is founded upon principles that recognize the supremacy of God and the rule of law"… and continue to wonder what it really means for each and every citizen of this blessed land

July 2

Did I (on May 22nd) say the mask is being too politicized? "Experts have clashed over research into the efficacy of wearing masks (even homemade face coverings) in public. There is no question that public health experts have at times given confusing guidance on mask-wearing. The authorities were aware that as the COVID-19 outbreak continued to spread and expand globally, the supply chain for these devices would be stressed if demand exceeded available supplies. But what about it now? Has the attitude about face masks changed and become too politicized? It seems face masks have now become a political football in the age of COVID-19. Despite the controversy, May continues to make them, and it is a good thing!"…

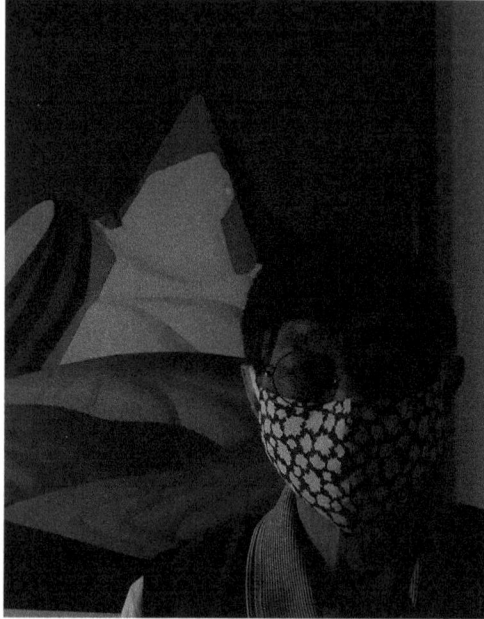

July 5

Dominant Coronavirus Strain Appears to Be a Mutated, More Virulent Version, Study Finds… "It's more of a live look into science unfolding: an interesting discovery was made that potentially touches millions of people, but we don't yet know the full scope or impact."
- https://www.sciencealert.com/current-dominant-strain-of-covid-

July 6

I suspect many of us must be wondering, when the mobs tore down a statue of Ulysses S. Grant, whether the "protesters" had ever learned anything in their high schools, colleges or universities. Could they know the name "Gettysburg" or even identify the century in which the Civil War was fought? Many of them seem to be in their 20s and 30s. But they appear to me to be juvenile delinquents, compared with those of my generation and World War II survivors. Schools, colleges, and universities are certainly teaching our students to be proud, confident, loud, and self-righteous.

I saw live on T.V. (and social media) in these last several weeks of lawlessness, riots, looting, and "cancel culture" revealed to me a poorly educated, fractious, petulant generation, and self-assured without reasons or justifications. How can this generation coming after us, so sheltered (with prolonged adolescence) yet claim to be all-knowing? Ask questions like these, and the answers will ultimately lead back to the schools, colleges, and universities?… The moral of this is not to leave the children and everything entirely to the education system.

July 9

Perhaps most of the problems we see in our societies (particularly in western societies) are due to our inability to recognize the meaning of "household" (as distinguished from the meaning of "family"). Three words on "household" are found in the Bible where the family is indicated. These three are the Hebrew word "bayith" and the Greek words "oikia" and "oikos". The "family" is intrinsic to the human condition. "Family" is the basic cell of all human society and forms the root of human relationships. The mutual influence and inevitable tensions of the "family" extend throughout the political philosophy of ancient Greek philosophers Plato and Aristotle. Human instinct draws a man and woman together to form a "family." The "household" turns this instinct into an ongoing form of life. John Cuddeback

A person can be part of a family without being part of the household. The "household" is a family understood as a community of daily life. Family has its root in the household. This means the "household" is properly the subject of rights, duties, and obligations. It is in the "household" that nature has done her best to offer us common life. "The decline of the family begins with the demise of the household"- John Cuddeback

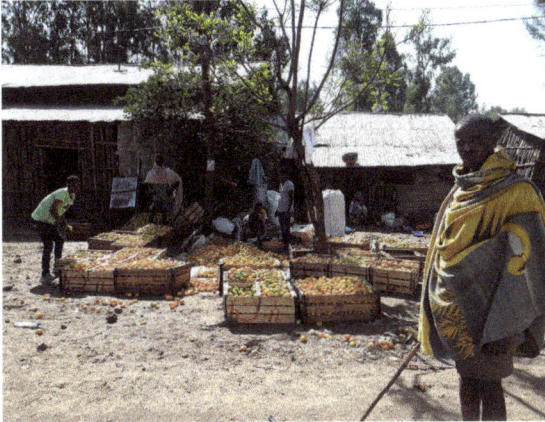

July B

In this challenging time of COVID-19, we share the importance of emotional honesty. I discovered how sharing my thoughts had helped me in trying to process what has happened. I am grateful to those who have helped in this process.

The fallout and ripple effect of the tragic case of George Floyd (May 25th, 2020) continues with the ongoing "Cancel Culture." This "Movement" had already covered up memorials and statues erected more than a century ago and had looked for ways to remove them permanently. Sin brought slavery (as we understand this "slavery") to America. Covering up our sin (with fig leaves like Adam and Eve) and destroying statues, and declaring that "Black Lives Matter" will never undo the sin. The slogan "Black Lives Matter" itself carries a racist tone and will not heal whatever wounds remain. Identity politics is an

"Awakening" without understanding and without forgiveness. Identity politics is divisive and will not purify the darkened hearts.

Many have written that America is "structurally" and "systemically" racist. We are all sinners with darkened hearts. However, if we label a country as racist and say racism "systemic," it ignores and understates the bad people's responsibility. The root cause of racism is sin. It is because all human beings are, to some extent ethnocentric, this sin is difficult to avoid. Racism damages the harmony and oneness that should characterize all our relationships. We do not have to fear our differences. Even what divides us does not have to destroy us. St. Paul tells us "be ye kind one to another, tenderhearted, forgiving one another, even as God for Christ's sake hath forgiven you": Ephesians: 4:32 (KJV). The dark gods of Identity politics, no doubt, will continue to haunt us. Much more than a fig leaf is needed to heal a darkened heart. We can pray for the grace to look beyond our own prejudices…

July 24

Civility and Civilization… Violent anarchy continues with riots, violence, and destruction for almost two months. There is defenestration of "civilitas" in those "liberal" cities in America where liberalism has gone nasty. Civility comes from Latin "civilitas." In early use, the term denoted the state of being a citizen and hence good citizenship or orderly behavior. We would think we are now living in a civilized country of the First (1st) World. You can chronicle a civilization; you can put dates on civilization. Not so with civility.

Civility is a way of being and not a thing. Civility is securely grounded in the aspiration for the common good. It is the virtue from which civilization flows. It is opposed to barbarity. "Civilitas" assumes devotion by the people, by the citizenry, especially as to the imparting of shared responsibility for the common good, a common purpose, and a sense of community. Everyone is obligated to observe "civilitas" if the community is to exist...

July 27

"There is, for better or worse, a predictability in our lives, a stability of choice, an ingrained disposition to act in one way rather than another" - Ralph McInerny on the Moral philosophy of Thomas Aquinas.

In observing what is happening in societies (particularly the nasty and destructive "liberalism" in America), I do believe we have, very significantly, if not completely, lost our understanding and comprehension (both theoretically and practically) of virtue. What is virtue? We may ask ourselves. Is it a keystone and cornerstone to life and civilization? Should all parents and educators make every effort to understand the need for growth in virtue and character formation? I do not pretend to know the answer. "But speak thou the things which become sound doctrine: That the aged men be sober, grave, temperate, sound in faith, in charity, in patience." Titus 2:1-2 (KJV).

May we (who are followers of Christ) be reminded of these: "But thou, O man of God, flee these things; and follow after righteousness, godliness, faith, love, patience, meekness." 1 Timothy 6:11 (KJV)… "And let the peace of God rule in your hearts, to which also ye are called in one body: and be ye thankful." Colossians 3:15 (KJV)… So be it!

July 28

Are we daft about political correctness? It is observed that a man, especially a white man, is constantly haunted by the fear of being viewed as racist. He has to walk on eggshells for fear of unwittingly transgressing on political correctness. A black manager is afraid of being perceived as misogynistic if he gives honest and critical feedback to his white female subordinate. For more than ten years, a youngster who had known me finally gathered the courage to ask whether I am Korean. His parents had always used the generally accepted politically correct term "Asian" …Is political correctness making fools and cowards of us all?

"Christianity thinks of human individuals not as mere members of a group or items in a list, but as organs in a body - different from one another and each contributing what no other could"… C.S. Lewis says that there are two ways that the Christian mindset can be corrupted. If people think of themselves as utterly different from one another, without any common bond of religion, then they become individualists. If, however, they come to think that all people are just the same, their way of thinking becomes Totalitarian. Christianity, and Christianity alone, defines human beings as different yet also united - any step toward Totalitarianism or individualism is a dangerous perversion of the faith…

"I have a dream that my four little children will one day live in a nation where they will not be judged by the color of their skin, but by the content of their character." :- Martin Luther King Jr.

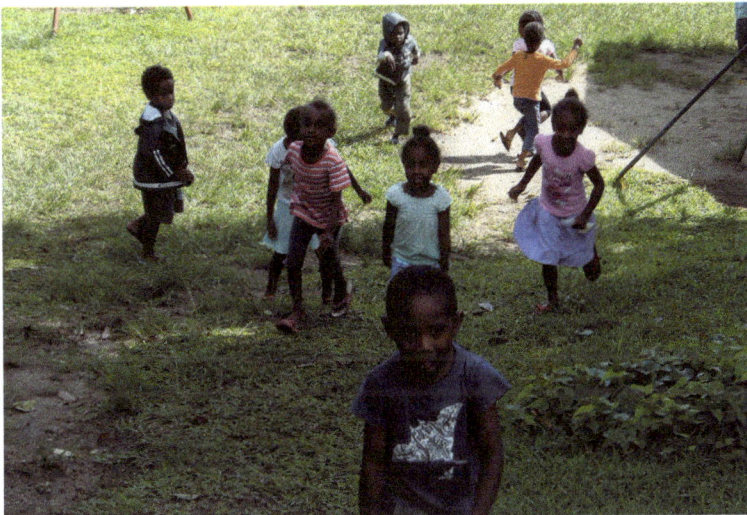

August 3

There is Hope, Peace, Joy, and Love. But first, we need to seek. We need to ponder. We need to feel about the importance of asking the big questions to which there may be no easy answers. However, in almost every discipline (we are aware of) in our education system, materialistic understanding of humanity seems to dominate. God, free will, meaning, and purpose have become pejorative terms in schools, universities, and academia. Richard Dawkins has put it that "Darwin made it possible to be an intellectually fulfilled atheist." Cosmos (Kosmos) has replaced the Creator and our minds subsumed by "matter". We are imbued with reverence for the materialistic!

Who is the "mind" behind the minds at the reliefs of Ra'meses, the inscribed steles of Assyrian kings, the Michelangelo paintings on the ceiling of the Sistine Chapel, in the high-tech environments in our modern era and even in the writing of this post? We can choose the way or indeed whether even to ponder… Which way? …

August 4

I have been reading with interest the removal of Christopher Columbus's statues (particularly the one from Columbus, Ohio) and recall my own journey to the New World (Mundus Novus). The reason for the removal of the statue? "For many people in our community, the statue represents patriarchy, oppression, and divisiveness. That does not represent our great city, and we will no longer live in the shadow of our ugly past," - Mayor Andrew Ginther.

I am informed that some historians had even invented a progressive Columbus myth for several reasons. This one is perhaps another one of the hoaxes and will be perpetrated by revisionists. Is it possible that some like to make this Catholic Genoese navigator an unlikely American progressivist hero? We have all read about the vague claim that Christopher Columbus proved to a dark and disbelieving late-medieval Europe that the world is not flat. But any educated person in medieval Europe already knew that. Some have thought it crucial to portray religion (particularly Christianity) as a reactionary force and an opponent of modern enlightenment and Darwinism. Perhaps some still hate the Spanish Empire and Roman Catholicism. This snowball effect which started centuries ago has grown to outrageous proportions …

August 5

Legend has it that Xi Shi was an ancient beauty so entrancingly beautiful that fish would forget to swim and sink when she walks by... If we think we are being victimized, we can be overwhelmed with an infinite variety of ugliness less attractive than Xi Shi's variety. This is a cause for pause.

Think about what is going on in the current lawlessness and mayhem in our societies. Are these the unintended "fruits" of the thought of "victimization"?... It is simply irresponsible to teach children that they can expect their salvation to lie in slogans like "Black Lives Matter" or other flights of rhetoric. As always, this expectation is further complicated by hyperboles and destructions, which give away a lot of the common good but gain extraordinarily little for the individual. Clarence Thomas, the African American (black) Supreme Court judge, said during an on-stage interview at the Library of Congress in Washington: "At some point, we're going to be fatigued with everybody being the victim".

The "victim" suffers from the repetitiveness of his own condition, a vicious cycle, making him unable to change and be transformed. This repetitiveness threatens him even further when "victimization" is transmuted into a form of public entertainment (enlisting public sympathy) with plenty left over for the "journalists" on T.V. and news outlets. This modern "awakening" (of universal victimization) has resulted in cynicism and "despair," which prompted a section of the American population towards the vengeful display of aggression, lawlessness, indiscriminate and desecratory violence (which are still ongoing) supposedly linked to the wicked killing of George Floyd on May 25th, 2020.

August 10

Forgiveness cleanses us…Some of us will look all the way back to the time of cain and abel to find faults and ills in humanity. Some of us will look for moments of "hurt" or "wrong" (sometimes even vicariously in centuries and decades past) so we feel "victimized. "Others will let go, move on and find peace …I am not trying to put the old wine into a new bottle when i quote paul boese: "forgiveness does not change the past, but it does enlarge the future." The peace prayer of st. Francis of assisi reads: "lord, make me an instrument of your peace: where there is hatred, let me sow love; where there is injury, pardon…".

Jesus taught us to pray: "and forgive us our sins as we forgive those who sin against us". This verse presupposes universal sinfulness. We are all sinners, even though some of us may not realize. Everyone, no matter how holy, have sins which need to be forgiven. However, the petition in the lord's prayer does not stop with "forgive us our sins" but continues with "as we forgive those who sin against us."

It is not easy for us to forgive others to the point where we are at peace and when we actually feel ourselves cleansed of bitterness and resentment and are praying for those who "hurt" and "victimize" us. I do not pretend to be able to do or have the answer. But I believe when we do, miracle happens! We are transformed. Every miracle depends on our relationship with god. That relationship is built strictly on the strength of his forgiveness of our sin. Sins can be present in us, but it is the absence of forgiveness which comes between us and god. Forgiveness is the key: - Matthew 18:21-35 and Matthew 6:14-15.

August 17

Moral compass... Presently we have two ways in this "world." Each going in the opposite direction, with those travelling thereon continuing to jeer and badmouth each other. "But those things which proceed out of the mouth come forth from the heart, and they defile the man." :- Matthew 15:18 (KJV).

Ask not whether we are travelling on the extreme left or on the extreme right. Ask what our moral compass is! Does being moderate mean standing in the middle of the highway? Not at all! This is false. It is, at any rate, a bad picture. It is for each person to define his Way, guided by his moral compass.

The problem is that (if ideology evolves in a person) "self-knowledge" comes late. This may be for the BETTER or for the WORSE. By the time we think we know ourselves, we are no longer what or where we were. We may no longer recognize our own selves. It is good if our ideology has evolved for the common good. The disaster comes if it is the opposite. The question is who and where are we?... Who and where we are in the world, both physically and ideologically, says a great deal about how we see the world...?

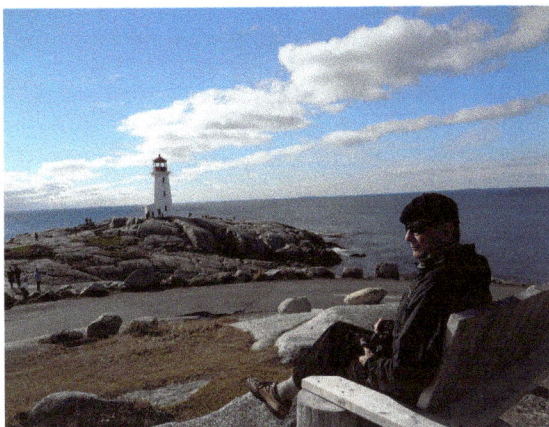

August 24

All lives matter! ... as observed through a simple lens... "No one is born hating another person because of the color of his skin," which became the most-liked tweet of former president Barack Obama as he quoted Nelson Mandela in response to the white supremacist march in Charlottesville. However, according to a body of scientific research on human development, the average infant will automatically begin to distrust anything that looks and sounds different than their parents at around six (6) months:- The Other-Race Effect Develops During Infancy (Sage Journals on psychological science). "Parents do not teach children to be biased" - Kang Lee, a human development researcher at the University of Toronto… It is because of this "default setting," children (humans) need to learn and practise the Second Great Commandment!

The Second Great Commandment is "Thou shalt love thy neighbour as thyself.": - Matthew 22:39. The journey (with the focus on this Commandment) is one which most of us are constantly struggling in… C.S. Lewis puts it like this: "Do not waste time bothering whether you love your neighbour; act as if you did. As soon as we do this, we find one of the great secrets. When you are behaving as if you loved someone, you will presently come to love him." … Instead of trying to follow Jesus's Teachings and Lewis's advice, some (as observed through my simple lens) insist we are in a battle for "the better angels and the soul" by promoting the poison of unforgiveness; by bad-mouthing others; by encouraging hatred; by supporting slogans of divisions; by emboldening "protestors" to violence, causing the destruction of properties, monuments, and churches; by condoning unrest, mayhem, and deliberate killings; by snuffing out the lives of the unborn, the innocent, and the defenseless … "What Do I Believe and Why Does It Matter?". Christians have been taught to Think Like Jesus. … Still, some of us look to our political leaders for (and take them as) the moral compass. Others, in good conscience by faith, believe in, and accept the guidance of the Paraclete …What do we really believe in?

August 31

Just one Chinese Canadian perspective…On this coming Sunday, four hundred years ago (September 6, 1620 o.s.) the English ship Mayflower set sail from the port of Plymouth, England. She transported the first English Puritans, known today as the Pilgrims, from England to the New World. Plymouth (Massachusetts) and Jamestown (Virginia) symbolize the beginnings of "America" from an English-Speaking point of view. John Rolfe, Virginia's first tobacco grower and husband of the Red (as distinguished from East) Indian princess Pocahontas, wrote in a letter to the Virginia Company of London (in the widely held account of the African landing in America) stating that the captain of a warship that arrived in Jamestown in August 1619 "brought not anything but 20 and odd Negroes, wch the Governor and Cape Marchant bought for victuale…". The year 1619 is (currently) revisited with the launching of the "1619 Project" in great fanfare. The Project's self-proclaimed goal is to convince the Americans that the nation's "true founding" occurred not in 1776 but in 1619 when 20 or so slaves came ashore in the Jamestown colony to "reframe" American history around slavery and the contribution of African Americans.

The United States of America was created on July 4, 1776, with the Declaration of Independence of thirteen (13) British colonies in North America. Ignoring the idea of America's first (?) slaves is probably not historically correct? The past speaks for itself, and history is more than "the crimes and misfortunes of the human race." Narratives associated with the "1619 Project" only posit a colonial past. Invoking a part of history (which is subject to misconceptions and debates) to support one's argument is, strictly speaking, a risky and dangerous exercise. At this point in time, when we invoke history, we are in the future and not in the past. Any narratives for the purpose of "reframing" the concept that America is not a nation founded on freedom, equality, and opportunity but founded by slavery, inequality, and racism are harmful, to say the least. Invoking this is indeed distortive and distracting to the effort of thinking through a shared future. Selective memories are not useful if the desire and goal is to work towards a free, pluralistic, and just society +++

September 7

As the date approaches, some of us are still being reminded of the violent events of 9/11 and continue to discern how/whether we can bring the "darkness" into the light. Before the Enlightenment, Christian theology (in the Augustinian tradition) provided the dominant paradigm for interpreting evil. In an interesting thought experiment, St. Augustine imagines two persons of equal intellectual and emotional disposition of whom one gives in to temptation while the other resists it; from this, he concludes that the difference must be due to a free, spontaneous, and irreducible choice of the will- St. Augustine (De civitate Dei).

We understand and are not confused with the terms "conscious" and the term "conscience." They refer to hugely different things. To be conscious is our awareness of ourselves and the world around us. Our conscience is our ability to distinguish between what is right and what is wrong, what is good and what is evil. Our consciousness allows us to be aware of who we are, our place in society and in the world, while our conscience allows us to feel and behave in moral, ethical, and acceptable ways. In our thinking, it is not adequate to accept evil as a mystery. It must be explained, understood, and accepted according to human reason, or else it goes against the human spirit. C.S. Lewis says, "Evil is a parasite, not an original thing." It is goodness spoiled! "Understanding what is evil" is the purpose of our existence. "Understanding what is evil" makes us worthy of having goodness, love, and joy as we travel along this life-long journey...

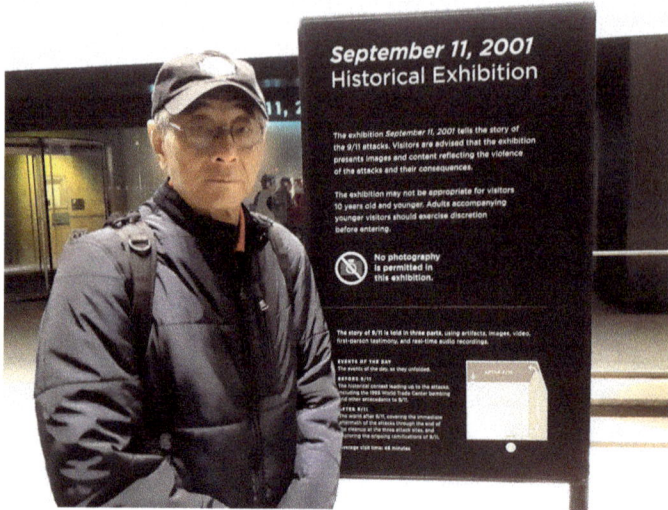

September 11

Forgive me on this day that I need to have a chat
About the time when we fallen men were truly bad
The selfless heroes and the innocents are dead
While "Darkness" in the world is still widespread
I did travel from afar to pay them the due respect
But this is a moment in time we should all reflect
On the awful death, they suffered in this violent crime
No day shall erase them from the memory of time
These heroes and the innocents had lived with love
And ascended into heaven as gentle spiritual doves…

September 14

When I saw myself in a dark cave, I thought of the devil. We face a curious predicament when we think of the Devil... In 1821, Friedrich Schleiermacher already stated the case bluntly: - "The idea of the devil as developed among us is so unstable that we cannot expect anyone to be convinced of its truth." In this modern time of the internet, smartphone, Creative Cloud, and Artificial Intelligence, do we still think of the devil? Can we still talk about the Devil? Apprehend him in thought? However, for us to expurgate the Devil is to ignore the critical aspect of reality and for those of us who are Christians to forget the Christian tradition "sive Diabolus, nullus redemptor" (without the Devil, there is no Redeemer). Only by grasping the Evil One's depth (in a previous post, I mentioned "Understanding what is evil") can we know the goodness and the full extent of the love of God.

The truth is the Devil is real. The Devil is the evil and contemptuous trickster who works to create conflicts among us, cause strife, consume us in doubt, fear, worry, and lure us to do the wrong things. He seeks to divert and catch us in a tangled web of images, the ultimate effect of which gives us false pride, and for Christians, the loss of our faith.

The darker aspect of human (nature) life does not have to remain in the dark. We know that we can bring ourselves to the surface … to the light! We do not have to remain as frogs in a well. The Chinese say:- "A frog in a well cannot discuss the ocean… A summer insect cannot discuss ice…" (井蛙不可以語於海者…夏蟲不可以語於冰者…) To use Plato's famous image, we live in a cave, mistaking shadows for reality. We need to climb out of the darkness, adjust our eyes as we appear in the illuminating light in search of "Epignosis"

September 22

We are indeed living in a different time… A verse every Christian commits to memory is Matthew 6:33 (KJV): "But seek ye first the kingdom of God, and his righteousness, and all these things shall be added unto you." This phrase, "The Kingdom of God," has been in the news recently given Amy Coney Barrett's reported use of the phrase. She appears on President Trump's shortlist of nominees to replace Ruth Bader Ginsburg who died last week. Her language of building the kingdom of God has made some people uncomfortable…

Is it true that for those of us who are making the journey (and for no others) that the Kingdom of God is everywhere? "But what, you ask, of the earth? Earth, I think, will not be found by anyone to be, in the end, a very distinct place. I think earth, if chosen instead of Heaven, will turn out to have been, all along, only a region in Hell: and earth, if put second to Heaven, to have been from the beginning a part of Heaven itself." ... Is it harmful that Jesus taught us to pray: "Thy kingdom come, Thy will be done on earth, as it is in heaven"

September 22

"We are what we read. We are also what we eat". Even though this thought is utterly personal and rooted in the particular circumstances at this stage of my life, I have made a choice to share it:- ... I recall quoting a line by Ralph Waldo Emerson: - "I cannot remember the books I've read any more than the meals I have eaten even so they have made me" @ http://www.freepilgrim.com/new-world/

I have always wondered what C S Lewis meant when he wrote: "Literary experience heals the wound, without undermining the privilege, of individuality... in reading great literature I become a thousand men and yet remain myself. Like the night sky in the Greek poem, I see with a myriad of eyes, but I still see it. Here, as in worship, in love, in moral action, and in knowing, I transcend myself; and am never more myself than when I do."? We are reading our favorite books or e-books (perhaps more likely are watching our favorite social media). We think we are always learning. However, we never come to the knowledge (Epignosis) of the truth... But here is the truth about the Good Book:- "All scripture is given by inspiration of God, and is profitable for doctrine, for reproof, for correction, for instruction in righteousness:"- 2 Timothy 3:16 (KJV)

People in the Third World are struggling to find food. Many do not have the choice to eat what they like. In our so-called 1st World (the West with Judeo-Christian heritage) we forget we have been blessed with abundance. We eat what we like (sometimes too much) but are we eating the right food, having a balanced diet? Can we ward off clogged arteries, high blood pressure, high cholesterol, obesity, and diabetes? I do not pretend to know the answer... but I give thanks for being able to choose what to eat...

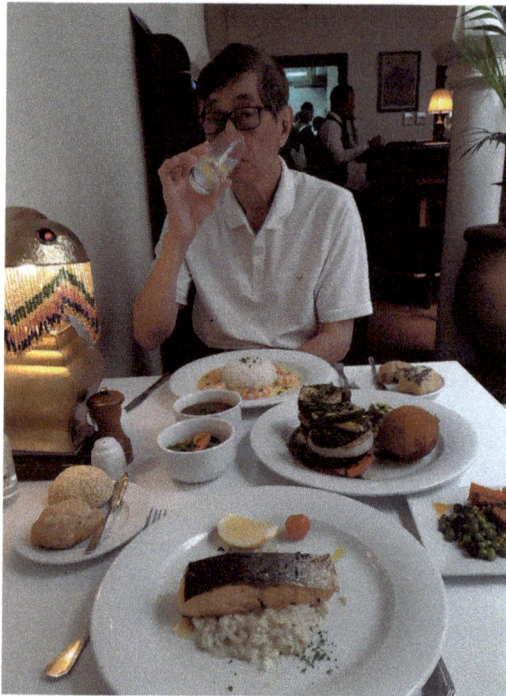

September 27

A couple of decades ago, Charles John Sommerville wrote: "How The News Makes Us Dumb: The Death Of Wisdom In An Information Society"...

Do not judge does not mean having no opinion. We are not to judge (in the sense of condemn), but we are compelled to judge (in the sense of discerning). We should be able to see and judge what is right and what is wrong. We can tell the content of the character of a person by what he sees in others. The "dishonest" persons (reporters, journalists, and media personnel in particular) only see the bad side, with none of the good side, of another person. Going by this principle of the "dishonest" persons, King David's story would have ended with Bathsheba. However, history and experience show us that there is still goodness in humanity despite our sinful attributes (Adam's Fall). But it appears we are now living in a culture that thrives on looking for things that are wrong with others - particularly by the "liberal" press and "news" networks. Just read the "news" and watch the broadcasts and comments on major "news" networks (without self-deception) and you will understand what I mean. We can indeed call out: "Sir, you perhaps, are not lying, but you are not telling the whole truth. It is not the same thing - this is like a knockoff Louis Vuitton"!

The Evil One deceives us into identifying ourselves with (and limiting us to) our dishonest attributes. But we can also be much more than our sinful attributes. We do not need to go all the way back to ancient time to understand the concept of "Limitedness". Jean-Paul, in recent time, pointed us to this idea. He explained that people limited themselves through their life choices: "On est ce qu'on veut" (we are what we want). Human beings (reporters, journalists, media personnel included) can "change." I try to avoid "born again" a term which many consider pejorative in current culture. But the timing of the challenge to Amy Coney Barret's "Kingdom of God" appears to me to be such "a coincidence." Jesus said: "Verily, verily, I say unto thee, except a man be born again, he cannot see the kingdom of God."-John 3:3 (KJV). We all have the potential to be transformed even though our sin has weakened our Free Will. Our Free Will (if it chooses) will resist grace...

September 30

Believest thou this?... It is all a matter of perspectives (correct or wrong) depending on whom we choose to guide (lead) us - the One in the Light (Paraclete) or the One in the Dark (Evil One). "And God said, this is the token of the covenant which I make between me and you and every living creature that is with you, for perpetual generations: I do set my bow in the cloud, and it shall be for a token of a covenant between me and the earth. And it shall come to pass, when I bring a cloud over the earth, that the bow shall be seen in the cloud: And I will remember my covenant, which is between me and you and every living creature of all flesh; and the waters shall no more become a flood to destroy all flesh" : Genesis 9:12-15 (KJV).

Whenever I see a rainbow, I remember the Covenant God made with Noah. However, at the same time, when I see the rainbow, I would be thinking: God did not include "fire" in the Covenant? + … Then I see huge and uncontrollable fire and smoke, and I "foolishly" refer to what Jesus said, "But the same day that Lot went out of Sodom it rained fire and brimstone from heaven and destroyed them all." Luke 17:29 … What did Jesus mean by that?… Perhaps this verse is good for us who are professing the Christian faith "to think with"…? Are we followers of Christ? Who is our Guide?

October 5

"Culture is the root of politics, and religion is the root of culture."— *Richard John Neuha*

Growing up in Sibuga I did not know of a (special) Thanksgiving Day. Many years later (as we were celebrating Thanksgiving Holidays), someone informed me that the first thanksgiving feast took place in 1619. The Pilgrim Fathers (settlers of Plymouth Colony in America) invited the Indians (Red as distinguished from East Indians, known today as Native Americans) to join them in a three-day feast of wild turkey, venison and vegetables.

Next Monday, October 12, 2020, will be Thanksgiving Day for Canadians. In Canada, Thanksgiving has been celebrated as an annual holiday since November 6, 1879. It was officially proclaimed (on January 31, 1957) by Governor-General Vincent Massey as "A Day of General Thanksgiving to Almighty God for the bountiful harvest with which Canada has been blessed – to be observed on the Second Monday in October."

I grew up with Religious Knowledge as a lesson in Sung Siew School and was blessed with a distinction on this subject in the Senior Cambridge School Leaving Certificate (GCE) Examinations ... Is religious knowledge harmful? To me, there is constitutionally no reason for the school curriculum to exclude the teaching of religious studies or to discourage/prohibit religious discourse (wrongly assumed as religious bigotry) in the lives of many of our citizens relating to the founding of a country. The foundation of Thanksgiving comes from the Psalms: "Enter into his gates with thanksgiving, and into his courts with praise be thankful unto him and bless his name. For the Lord is good; his mercy is everlasting, and his truth endureth to all generations." Psalms 100: 4-5 (KJV) ... So, let us rejoice in the coming celebration of this Bible-based holiday of Thanksgiving.

October 8

Understanding and Knowing... A moderate knows he is not very good, but a really bad person thinks there is nothing wrong with himself - it is always the other's fault. When a sick person is getting better and better, he understands more and more clearly what is wrong that is still left in him. However, if he is getting worse, he understands his own illness less and less. This is common sense, really. We understand what sleep is when we are awake, not while we are asleep. We can understand the nature of drunkenness when we are sober, not when we are drunk...

October 11

Have you had meals with your friends? … Most of us know a lot of people but very few we can call friends, let alone best friends. Most people like to say "my friend so and so…" even though they may not fully comprehend what a "friend" is… Most so-called friendship is superficial, and friends are really mere acquaintances. But humour me: Try to think of the first best friend you have ever had. Do you remember what that friendship was first based on?

We are created for relationships with God and with others. This "relationship thing" is a gift from God. We all are known to God (although some of us may not have a relationship with Him). God said to Moses: "Certainly I will be with thee". Exodus 3:12 (KJV). But with humans, we have to be known by others through relationships. This relationship is rooted in friendship. Friendship perhaps arises when two or more companions discover that they have something in common. Something they thought was unique to themselves until they discovered the other person's similar mix of shared interests, shared values, and kindred spirits (someone they could click with).

But first, we need to be connected, discovered, and known by others in order to form "friendship".

There is something human in us that makes us want to be connected, be discovered, be known, have a relationship, belong, and understand. We can tell who our friends are (when we write to them or have a conversation with them) by their response by looking at their faces, observing their attention level, or even their laughter or intelligent silence at our humor. The response and "language" or the lack thereof say a lot about how our message is coming across in the "friendship"... whether there is a "relationship" or whether the "relationship" will totter and fall...

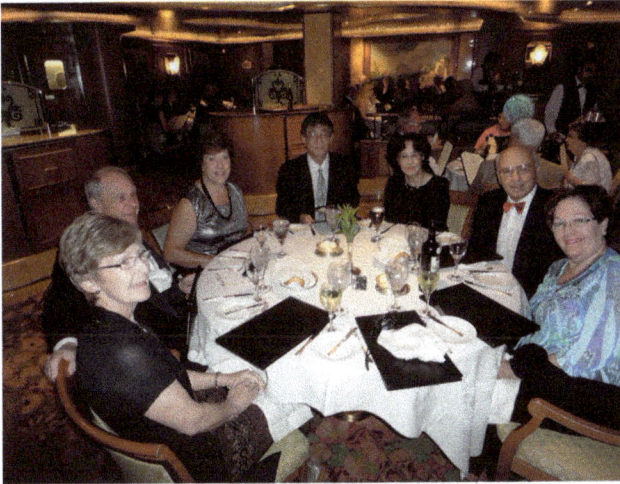

October 18

The Narrow Way less travelled ... Here in the West, is my fear, that the popular Individualism of unrestrained personal liberty trumps the common good. The individual has the tendency to act without reference to others, particularly in matters of lifestyle choices and social actions. However, in another aspect, the culture has swung to the tragic opposite: Individual freedom of speech is suppressed, blocked or banned. BIG Tech companies and dishonest media control/hide the truth (?). Do we deserve to know? But they are at liberty to facilitate or dish out "news" which attack, mock and demonize people of faith. How do we judge (discern) the content of the character of people? Debates will undoubtedly continue, with some insisting they are fighting for "the better angels and soul" of the nation. Those who believe and understand this is a dangerous perversion of the Christian faith ...

We can learn from C.S. Lewis: "I feel a strong desire to tell you - and I expect you feel a strong desire to tell me - which of these two errors is the worse. That is the devil getting at us. He always sends errors into the world in pairs - pairs of opposites. And He always encourages us to spend a lot of time thinking which is the worse. You see why, of course? He relies on your extra dislike of the one error to draw you gradually into the opposite one. But do not let us be fooled. We have to keep our eyes on the goal and go straight through between both errors. We have no other concern than that with either of them" ... There are different paths in life; different ways so to speak. We all, by grace, can walk on the Narrow Way. But many (who choose to resist grace) will not search for the Narrow Way or find it in vain. Some will tell us that we are fools because the Narrow Way is not easy to walk on ...

Jesus tells us to make a wise choice of the path we follow in this life: "Enter ye in at the strait gate: for wide is the gate, and broad is the way, that leadeth to destruction, and many there be which go in there at: Because strait is the gate, and narrow is the way, which leadeth unto life, and few there be that find it" - Matthew 7:13-14 (KJV)... ("Enter through the narrow gate. For wide is the gate and broad is the road that leads to destruction, and many enter through it. But small is the gate and narrow the road that leads to life, and only a few find it").

October 28

I just had the original battery of my Mercedes Benz 2012 model replaced and was advised by a supervisor at MB Vancouver that I must drive my car at least 300 KMs a month to keep the new battery "healthy". I believed and understood what he said. So, I had to go for a drive to "nowhere" in this pandemic situation. Then I was thinking about the necessary consumption of fossil fuel and the man-made effect on the environment, even though a minuscule of harm is done compared with the smoke and trees destroyed in the California fire (no pun intended).

Nothing here is against naturist/environmentalists who constantly engage in thoughts about nature, except, perhaps, they do not attend to the notion that they are producing such thoughts. For me, the fact that we are able to think indicates that something more than nature exists. This supernatural "thing" of us having the ability to think is not esoteric. How is it that we are doing it most of the time without even being conscious of it (like breathing)? However, as we go into the deeper level of "thinking," we begin to discern (and then we are able to judge). Then perhaps, (still perhaps) we can judge (discern) the content of the character of a person (including ourselves). But to discern our own character, we have to let humility take over the false ego and allow the Holy Spirit to fill the space of the 3rd person in us...With "discernment" and "revelation," we begin to realize our faults and flaws. If we believe and understand Saul of Tarsus's story and choose "transformation by grace," we will not let "Past behaviour dictate future behaviour"...

November 1

On this day honour all the saints, known and unknown and recall the words of St. Augustine: "Since you cannot do good to all, you are to pay special attention to those, who by accidents of time, or place, or circumstances, are brought into closer connection with you".

November 2

It is Spiritual Work of Mercy to pray for the souls of the departed, imploring God to purify the souls of the dead. On this All-Souls' Day, we pray for all the poor souls (of our dearly departed) who are languishing in the darkness that they may be sanctified. Believeth thou this?

November 4

The "Test" ... Mephistopheles is a demon featured in German folk-lore. He originally appeared in literature as the demon in the Faust legend. Shakespeare mentions "Mephostophilus" in The Merry wives of Windsor. By the 17th century, the "name" became independent of the Faust legend. According to Burton Russell: "That the name is a purely modern invention of uncertain origins makes it an elegant symbol of the modern Devil with his many novel and diverse forms." Although Mephistopheles appears to Faust as a demon - a minion of Satan - some are of the view that he does not search for men to corrupt but comes to collect the souls of those who are already damned.

Let us now step into one of the most mind-bending books in the Scripture: the Book of Job. No straightforward answers to all our big questions are found in this Book, but we are invited to ponder the pain and protestations of Job (Job 1-3, 19, 29-31), the puzzling and bewildering speeches of God (Job 38-41), and the surprising conclusion of the whole story (Job 42). Most people finish the Book feeling unsure they got the point. Perhaps they are convinced that they have experienced something profound.

The "Test" is the subject of the Book of Job. Satan wants (God) to test Job's faith because, according to Satan, Job's piety can be attributed only to the fact that Job has been blessed with prosperity. According to Satan, Job is a good servant of God because his faith has never been tested. People living under the Judeo-Christian heritage have been blessed with prosperity. Today, Satan says to God: "You have given them everything they could ever want: But put forth thine hand now ... and they will curse thee to thy face." God says to Satan: "Behold, they are in thine hand." So, God gives Satan permission to do whatever he likes to do with their lives ... What is going to be the conclusion of their stories?...

The Merry wives of Windsor: "Pist. How now, Mephostophilus" (Act I, Scene I, line 128). - The Complete Works of Shakespeare (Kittredge Players Illustrated Edition).

November 5

PRIDE - In the conclusion of http://www.freepilgrim.com/cultural-pilgrimage/, I posted the question: Is human conflict the "fruit" of the original sin (Pride) of man? For Christians, the doctrine of the Fall (Book of Genesis) is the only satisfactory explanation! God gave man the Free Will but the first sinner (Eve) preferred and chose a lesser good: Herself (Adam followed her) because there was nothing evil in the Garden of Eden for her to choose from. God was the greater good.

"Pride" is in fact our Fall. Freedom is real but it is not infinite. Once we have chosen ourselves over God, it reduces our freedom (we deprive ourselves) to choose anything else and the result is disastrous, as we have observed in the course of human history. We continue to observe conflicts in our societies today.=We (as Eve and Adam) "sink below freedom into the black fire of darkness" …

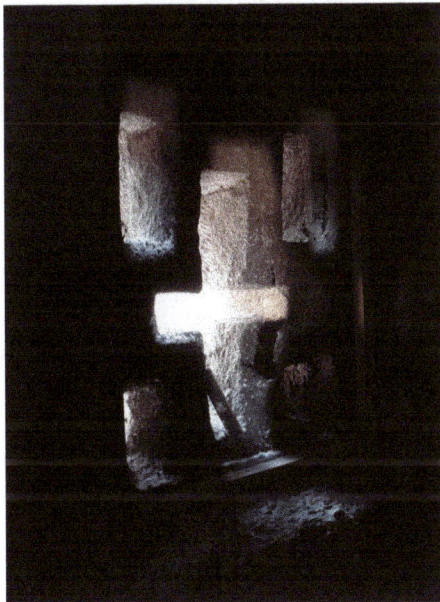

November 8

Are we really "woke"?… "And that, knowing the time, that now it is high time to awake out of sleep" - Roman 13:11 (KJV) … Is our society becoming increasingly secular or more? I believe the upshot has not been just "secularism" if by that term, we mean a culture of "dispassionate reason" that orders our common life. I believe that bowing at the feet of godless secularism has induced dishonesty. Are we becoming more and more dishonest? Is the truth being hidden from us by Tech companies and the media while Hollywood is entertaining us?

We are now living in a time when our "progressive" neighbours post new statements of "beliefs"! We are under the impression that a less "judgmental" culture or the absence of criticism would allow us to flourish in our "differences." However, on the contrary, we are now witnessing more and more hatred in our society, with increasing divisiveness and family instability among us. More people, especially the young, are experiencing anxiety, depressions, and diseases of despair… People are living under constant fear of being viewed as unkind, racist, homophobic, misogynistic, and religious bigots. Our hearts and souls are restless … It is not what we want, and it is not progress!

"Progress means getting nearer to the place you want to be. And if you have taken a wrong turn, then to go forward does not get you any nearer. If you are on the wrong road, progress means doing an about-turn and walking back to the right road; and in that case the man who turns back soonest is the most progressive man" —C.S. Lewis … May God reveals to us the truth as He did to the saints who have gone before us and those who are still living …

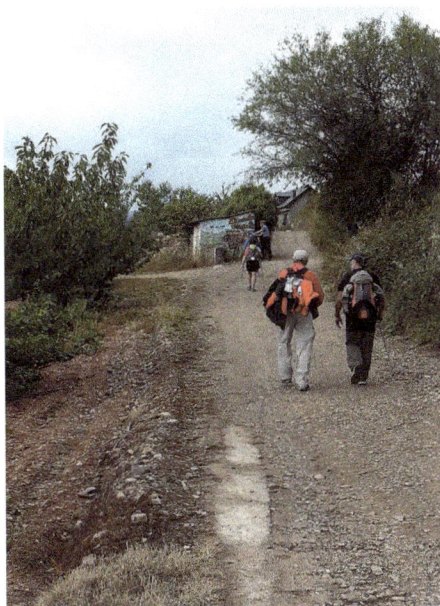

November 15

Three Kinds Of People... An old idea? No, not at all. I am not just referring to those who make things happen, those who watch things happen, and those who wonder (have no idea) what happened. As a Free Pilgrim, I have come to the growing awareness that there are also three other kinds of people. The first kind is those who simply live for their own sake with no consideration for others. They treat Man and Nature with contempt as merely raw material to be used in whatever way or form may serve them. The second kind is those who actually acknowledge and believe in some other claims upon them (the will of God, higher power, or common good). They believe in being a "good person," and they honestly try to pursue matters (in their own interests) no further than what they think these claims permit. They believe and give in to the higher claims as much as if paying their taxes and hope whatever is left over would be good enough for them to live by.

Their life is divided into "this is yours; this is mine." They live like school students "in class" and "out of class."

The last (rare and honest kind) are those who can (like the transformed Saul of Tarsus) say for them "to live is Christ." These are people who have got rid of the irksome business of choosing the rival claims of Self (first Eve) and God. They are rid of false ego and Self altogether. Their old egoists will have been made into a new thing that shines brightly outside the bushel. The will of Christ (last Adam) becomes theirs. In whatever they are gifted and called to do, they do so heartily with honesty. Their time, in belonging to Christ, also belongs to them, for they are His.

November 22

Contentment and joy…Some people (particularly those born in a time of war) understand what is getting along with humble means. They may have held high offices, lofty positions, lived in prosperity and luxury. They may have also learned the secret of being filled and going hungry; experienced both having the abundance and the suffering need; have had plenty of fun and occasional ecstasy but also have endured the sufferings of both physical and emotional pain. Many are asking these questions: "What are we looking for, and what is it that we want? What does a person need to do in order to find **contentment and joy** in this world?".

Once upon a time, the Chairman of a bank pointed to a friend, "See that?" He said: "Many years ago I used to sit there fishing. Every time I looked up here and wished I was in this penthouse. Now I look down and wish I was down there fishing"… Yet, we must pursue what we are called to do; to do our best to fulfill our purpose-driven life; heartily with integrity and honesty. Contentment does not mean complacency. We have to work hard to "better" ourselves. St. Paul says: "Art thou called being a servant? care not for it: but if thou mayest be made free, use it rather." -1 Corinthians 7:21 (KJV).

However, contentment can be an elusive pursuit. It depends on the quality of our thoughts. We go after what we think will make us happy and then find out we were happier before we started the quest. Contentment is not automatic nor a natural attitude but an acquired skill. For some, it is found and acquired through **contemplation** … To find and acquire contentment and joy, we need to be **truly** free and "If the Son, therefore shall make you free, ye shall be free indeed." - John 8:36 (KJV)… "Hitherto have ye asked nothing in my name: ask and ye shall receive, that your joy may be full" - John 16:24

Christmas & New Year Message...

COVID-19 Lockdown has deprived me of the opportunity to peregrinate but has given me more time to reflect. It is not harmful to us to read and meditate. It is even more helpful for us to proceed further with prayer and contemplation. Forsake 20-30 minutes of your screen time (in the early morning or late in the silence of the night) ... Nobody can make us joyful; not our company, not even our soulmate (for those of us who think we have one). However, if we have **joy,** we should share it (as a gift?) ... Like many, I used to walk around, looking only superficially and sensually at God's beautiful creation. I looked, but I never did really "see"! The "whole creation", in some way, has since had a profound effect on me as a Free Pilgrim ... It is because I care that I still hope you will walk with me...Believe and understand... Life can be enjoyed at a much deeper level (joy within us) than most people realize when there is no anger, anxiety, conflict, depression, jealousy, or other diseases of despair. I encourage everyone to go on a spiritual (if you will, a religious Camino/pilgrimage, not just a physical) journey. I believe each of us can be a discerning and complete (not good) person. We can never be good. "There is none good but one, that is, God."- Mark 10:18 (KJV) ... But "You are the salt and light of the world" ... Perhaps, in some way, you can make your life a gift to others ...

In preparation for Advent, I have decided to take a hiatus and await what the New Year will entail... with the hope that I may be doing something (behind the curtain) for the common good. Would we witness grace in the lives of our children and grandchildren and those coming after us? The answer would be very likely. The explosive nature of grace is unexplainable! A lot happened in 2020. For the first time since we landed in Canada, there will be no getting together (for us) here for Christmas. However, I hope (wherever we may be) we are still together in spirit, as one loving family ... I end here with our traditional Season Greetings: **"Merry Christmas and Happy New Year!"**

Photo (2014–10–24) taken of the Nativity scene carved out of an olive tree in Jerusalem.